What to
Talk About

WHAT
TO
TALK
ABOUT

On a Plane, at a Cocktail Party,
in a Tiny Elevator with Your Boss's Boss

by CHRIS COLIN *and* ROB BAEDEKER

illustrated by TONY MILLIONAIRE

CHRONICLE BOOKS
SAN FRANCISCO

Library of Congress Cataloging-in-Publication Data

Colin, Chris, 1975–
    What to talk about : on a plane, at a cocktail party, in a tiny elevator with your boss's boss / Chris Colin and Rob Baedeker ; illustrations by Tony Millionaire.
        pages cm
    Summary: "This hilarious yet practical manual written by two comedians tackles the fundamentals of good conversation, offering solid advice and sound social wisdom alongside faux-serious diagrams and inventories of real and humorously implausible scenarios"—Provided by publisher.
    ISBN: 978-1-4521-1450-7 (hardback)
    1. Conversation. 2. Conversation—Humor. I. Baedecker, Rob. II. Title.

    BJ2121.C59 2014
    818'.602—dc23

                                    2013032643

Manufactured in China.

Designed by Neil Egan
Additional typesetting and design by Liam Flanagan

10 9 8 7 6 5 4 3 2

Chronicle Books LLC
680 Second Street
San Francisco, California 94107
www.chroniclebooks.com

For to embetterment of talking.

CONTENTS

Introduction

IMAGINE almost any situation where two or more people are gathered—a wedding reception, a job interview, two off-duty cops hanging out in a Jacuzzi.

What do these situations have in common? Almost all of them involve people *trying to talk with each other.*

But in these very moments where conversation would enhance an encounter—where the right words would take an interaction to the next level—we so often fall short. We can't think of anything to say, or we can and it's rinky-dink, bush-league.

Even worse, we do a *passable* job at talking. We stagger through our romantic, professional, and social worlds with the goal merely of not crashing, never considering that we might soar. We go home sweaty and puffy and eat a whole birthday cake in the shower.

Deep down, we know there's more to human existence than just polite, prefabricated exchanges. We know that, with the right words, we can uncork new mysteries, discover new truths. Land better jobs. Get into some deep, soulful intercourse with a professor.

That's what *What to Talk About* is about to talk to you about. How about connecting with others in more interesting, unexpected ways? How about having a conversational "match" to spark conversation in any situation? Or a verbal "fire extinguisher" to hose down an interaction that's blown up in your face? How about putting people at ease? How about seeing others in new dimensions? How about adding some word-yarn to this giant salad-quilt we call the human experience?

* * * * *

There are simply no words to describe how important talking has been since the beginning of time. If there were a way to put all the conversations in history next to each other to form a string, that string could wrap around the Space Shuttle more than a billion times. It would have to, easily. Given this, you might think there was nothing left to say, but there is. And invariably, someone is waiting for you to say it.

Conversation is not only important for us humans. Scientists say that dolphins have been talking and giggling underwater this whole time, and we now know that elephants have twenty different words for "kfkjfs."

Yet consider the very researchers who study these animals—otherwise smart, successful men and women. Put them in a simple cocktail mixer and even the most basic conversations will jam them up, turn them to jelly.

And if the most learned and literate among us have such trouble, what chance do everyday, able-mouthed "normals" have?

Why is talking with other people so difficult?

It just is.

Quiz time. Do any of these situations sound familiar?

* I could spend an entire international flight worrying about an "opening line" for a conversation with the person sitting next to me.

* When someone attractive is flirting with me, my lips dry up and stick to my belt.

* I'm afraid if I correctly pronounce a fancy word like *bourgeois*, people will think I'm pretentious, and if I pronounce it incorrectly, people will think I'm *jejune*.

* I wish I could talk to my car mechanic, but she's too intimidating.

* I'm talkative and outgoing. I've heard people refer to me as "Mr. Trivia." Yet I rarely get invited to parties. WTF?

* At a social gathering where I don't know anyone, I "trip out" on my hands.

* When I gave the eulogy at my great-aunt's funeral, I took off my shirt.

Here's the good news: Even if you answered yes to all of the above, there's nothing wrong with you. Even you, top-less eulogy guy. We're all just capable people hitting normal potholes on the path to connecting with other people.

Maybe you're starting a new job, or maybe you're hoping to get that old job back. Maybe you're a new grad, keen to put your stamp on the world. Maybe you're looking to broaden your romantic possibilities, deepen your friendships, or brighten the silence at your family dinner table.

The first step is a mind-shift. Conversation doesn't have to be boring or awkward, banal or exhausting. Our interactions can be opportunities. They are gifts in which everyone can learn something new, in which everyone can give and receive, and in which everyone can feel a delicious human connection, even a powerful, erotic *frisson* (rhymes with "houseboat").

So lay back, open your body, and relax your mind. *What to Talk About* will give you the tools you need to succeed in any conversational situation. Over the course of this book you'll build a conversation "tool kit." With these tools, you become the spider, and your fellow conversationalists mere pawns in a chess game that somehow spiders are playing.

Perhaps some of these tools will be new to you. Perhaps others you already possess. But the question is, are you *using* them? If not, you're like a child drawing pictures of a train: You may be cute, but you're not a train conductor.

What to Talk About will give you the tools you need to drive the train or to shovel conversational "coal" into the . . . coal thing. You'll learn "openings" to help you insert yourself into even the most impenetrable conversations and the beautiful people having them. You'll learn the everyday pleasantries that grease the wheels of human interaction—and then how to go beyond them, whether you're at work or at home, at a party or on the road, on a date or at someone's death bed. You'll learn the secret routes to bypass awkward moments. You'll learn how to hit on your barista and talk with your parents on Skype. You'll learn how to pronounce *inchoate*.

What to Talk About is not rocket science, but it *is* a lot like brain surgery, in the sense that is terrifying, risky—and a ton of fun. It will also change your personality permanently. Let's go!

Chapter 1

Preparation and Openings

HOW TO PREFILL AN EMPTY MIND.

CASE STUDY: **Jerald**

A forty-four-year-old paralegal named Jerald P. describes himself as "fairly intelligent and good with people." On a Thursday night, he decided to go to a church-sponsored crab feed. Bravely, Jerald sat down at a picnic table with seven people he did not know. But after the introductory pleasantries were exchanged, an awkward silence fell over the group.

"I tried to think of something—anything—to say," remembers Jerald. "But my mind was blank. I ended up just fingering my crab and looking super close at those little hairs, sniffing the claws and getting some of their juices in my eyes."

Jerald thought of himself as "good with people," and even "fairly intelligent." But as the crab-feed disaster shows, average intelligence is not enough. One must also prepare. The great Mickey Mantle, the home run king, spent an hour each day waxing his bat. NOT FUN. But he did it. Every day. And he hated it. But he got to marry Marilyn Monroe. Nope. That was the other guy. See? Don't make assumptions.

The first principle of good conversation is to be ready for it. Know what you're going to talk about ahead of time. Most of us know to bring a bottle of wine to a dinner party, since it's bad form to arrive at a gathering empty-handed. So why would we ever arrive empty-*headed*?

"But hold on," you say. "What about all of the experience, education, instincts, and opinions that I've accumulated so far during my time on this planet. Isn't that enough preparation for a dinner party or awesome crab bake?"

You would think so. But remember those dolphin scientists? They were full of interesting knowledge, but when it came time to translate that knowledge into a real-life social situation involving humans, they just flailed around like rabbits in a bathtub. Good conversation begins not with you, but with the universe around you—ideas and things you discover and share.

Here's the great news: This book is packed with real, factual information that we got off the Internet or from old, hardbound almanacs that have been uploaded to the Internet. We've combed the world's database for conversation starters so you don't have to. For a full list, turn to the "Encyclopedia of Conversation Topics," page 147, where you'll find the sexiest, most up-to-date knowledge on subjects like the chuckwalla lizard, Silvio Berlusconi, and the nation of Eritrea. However, while accumulating material is the first step—one as vital as it is simple—it's even more important to know how to deploy that knowledge. That is where this chapter comes in.

To enter a conversation, you ideally want to connect to something someone else is saying. So first we'll look at "trigger words." But sometimes, if a hole doesn't open up in a conversation, you just have to blast one yourself, and this calls for "cold openings." Practice these, and in no time you'll be able to jump-start any discussion and drive it triumphantly through the streets of life.

TRIGGER WORDS

Let's say you've "prepared." You have come to the table with some fascinating and provocative data on a certain salt-snorting lizard that lives in the desert (see page 148). You're feeling good, crab all in your goatee and everyone's staring at you, thinking, "This guy *looks* like a beautiful genius, but what's he gonna *say*?"

Now what? You can't drop a statement like "the chuckwalla lizard, of course, never needs to drink water" on the table without any context. Everyone will just stare.

You need an *opening*, a link, a connection, a crack in the conversation into which you can insert yourself. The best way to do this is to pay attention for any reference in the current conversation that could be made to relate to your prepared material. We call this a "trigger word."

Here is an example:

> **Gorgeous Person:** "Would someone pass the *water*, please?"
>
> **You:** "I guess you're not a chuckwalla lizard."
>
> **Gorgeous Person:** "Excuse me?"

And you're in. For real impact, empty your pipe against the heel of your boot.

COLD OPENINGS

A trigger word ("water" in the conversation above) is the ideal way to enter a conversation. Not only does it make you seem like you're relating to the topic at hand, but you simultaneously appear to be listening. However, there are times when trigger words are hard to come by, such as when you're starting a conversation from scratch. In these cases, you need "cold openings"—bold, unboring statements that shoot you right past the usual pleasantries. Cold openings are meant to put people off-balance, but in a provocative way, so that they *fall back into you*, conversationally speaking. Here are some examples. Write them inside your waistband before the next mixer or use them as prompts to create your own:

Excuse me, do you have the app where you sigh loudly and your iPhone fixes whatever is bothering you?

I bet that a hundred years from now torture chambers will seem almost barbaric.

What URL do you think you want chiseled onto your gravestone?

Do you think train conductors get burned out on waving to people?

Weird how you never hear about ghosts appearing at the *gym*, right?

I bet there's a lot of eye-rolling at the triple-washed spinach factory right before round three.

Looks like the last person to use the toilet forgot to "log out."

[For women] My doctor just told me I'll never be able to grow a full beard.

I bet your spirit animal is an attic raccoon.

The original super-continent, Pangea, seems so obvious in hindsight!

You look like you just thought of something interesting.

You look like your mind just went blank.

You look like your mind just flipped over to AM radio.

If you got to have one additional eye, where would you want it located?

If you had an additional eye in the middle of your back, and you were online dating, would you mention it in your profile or wait till the first date?

Sometimes when I'm taking a shower I forget whether I've washed my hair. Is that normal?

Brazil nuts are bullshit. Just a big, bullshit nut.

You must be the only person in the world who doesn't love ice cream!

- If you're right, you will seem like a mind reader/sorcerer.

- If you're wrong, you can talk about how to get better at mind reading.

- If they love ice cream but are lactose intolerant, you can have a conversation about dairy-free ice cream products. And sorcerers.

Chapter 2

Small Talk

DON'T POOH-POOH IT. TAE-KWON-**DO-IT**.

CASE STUDY: **Raquel**

Raquel R., a graphic designer and aspiring artist, went to an album-release party for a friend of a friend. Everyone at the party was engaging in small talk—about the weather, their favorite bands, and so on—but Raquel wanted no part of it.

"Lame," thought Raquel, popping in earbuds and listening to her iTunes. "What a waste of time."

A week later, Raquel died in a skydiving accident.

Raquel didn't really die—she never existed. We invented her to teach you a lesson: Life is too short to judge other people or to write off opportunities to learn from them. (The consequences can be severe: It turned out one of the people at the party was so put off by Raquel's disengaged attitude that he actually booby-trapped Raquel's parachute. That part really happened.)

SMALL TALK

People dismiss small talk as superficial and boring. People are wrong. Small talk is an essential part of the social contract. It allows us to engage and identify common ground with safe, low-risk topics. Unlike the attention-grabbing antics of cold openings and trigger words, which jump-start a conversation or jolt it into more interesting territory, small talk is a gentle on-ramp. It uses banal or mundane topics as proving grounds where we can establish a comfy initial rapport with another person. Using small talk, we feel one another out and map the spots where we want to dig deeper.

Think about it: An offshore oil driller wouldn't just jam her wellbore into the seabed, willy-nilly. She'd survey the ocean floor, study the most likely spots to strike black gold, and then plunge past the crust. Same goes for conversation.

Here are three classic small-talk topics—traffic, prices, and the weather—with options for growing them into big talk.

SMALL TALK ABOUT TRAFFIC

Try talking about how the traffic on your way over was better or worse than usual. Empathize with the other person's agitation about having spent so much time in traffic, or share their delight in the lack of traffic where there should have been more.

Did you see any unusual vehicles along the way? E.g., classic cars, art cars, or maybe one of those hoarder cars packed with garbage where you can barely see the driver behind the wheel.

Talk about what you used to think about on the worst or best commute you ever had. Talk about the song your friend in Atlanta used to sing on her crappy commute. If you're feeling safe, call it "Hotlanta" like she does. (She was fun. What went wrong between you two, anyway?)

BIG TALK ABOUT TRAFFIC

* "Commute" comes from the Latin root *mutare*, meaning "to change." How do you think you change—physically, mentally, spiritually, karmically—during your daily commute?

* Do you know how to change a tire? Why or why not? What does that say about you? What does that say about tires?

* Which number is higher—the number of drivers you've flipped off, or the number of times you've been the flippee?

SMALL TALK ABOUT PRICES

Depending on the age, social position, and living situation of the person you're talking with, bring up how expensive gas/lattes/gum/pot/homes/apartments/hospice care have become. Talk about how things used to be cheaper. Talk about how much a movie star just paid for another movie star's mansion. Remember when movie stars used to live in their cars like everyone else?

Big Talk about Prices

* What's the best deal you've ever gotten? Got an especially good or especially terrible haggling technique? What was your most extravagant purchase ever?

* Do you ever think about moving somewhere with a lower or higher cost of living? Would you rather be considered "the Donald Trump of Allen, South Dakota," or "Bert the chimney sweep" of Londontown?

* Would you sleep with someone in this room— picked at random—for $375,000? If yes, try $374,000, and so on, till the answer changes. If no, try $376,000, and so on, until you find the sweet spot. It's fun to get this one down to the exact penny.

Small Talk about Weather

When it comes to small talk, weather is the eye of the storm! It's all around you, and changing fast. Talk about how cold/ hot it is right now, how cold/hot it's been, and how cold/ hot it might get. Connect the current weather or the forecast to an event you have coming up, and express hope that the weather doesn't interfere with that event.

BIG TALK ABOUT WEATHER

* What's the worst sunburn you've ever had?

* What's the coldest you've ever been? If you lost toes to frostbite, offer to show your feet.

* What's the worst storm you, or someone you know, has ever endured? What's the strangest weather phenomenon you've every witnessed? Would you rather freeze or burn to death?

* What, exactly, is wind? How does it know where to blow?

* What's the weather been like on the best days of your life? The worst day of your life?

* If there were no such thing as weather, what would take its conversational place?

* Ask, "If you had the opportunity to be struck by lightning, and it would hurt a lot but you'd survive with zero permanent damage to your mind or body, would you do it?" How much is an interesting experience worth to you?

ASK FOR STORIES,
NOT ANSWERS

Another way to get beyond small talk is to ask open-ended questions that invite people to tell stories, rather than give bland, one-word answers:

Instead of . . .	Try . . .
"How was your day?"	"What did you do today?"
"Where are you from?"	"What's the strangest thing about where you grew up?"
"What do you do?"	"What's your story?"
"What do you do?"	"What's the most interesting thing that happened at work today?"
"What line of work are you in?"	"How'd you end up in your line of work?"
"What's your name?"	"What does your name mean?" (If they say, "I don't know," reply, "What would you like it to mean?"

"How was your weekend?"	"What was the best part of your weekend?"
"How are you?"	"What are you thinking about right now?"
"What's up?"	"What are you looking forward to this week?"
"Would you like some wine?"	"Who do you think is the luckiest person in this room?"
"Nice to meet you."	"What does this house remind you of?"
"How long have you been living here?"	"If you could teleport by blinking your eyes, where would you go right now?"

BREAKING THE MIRROR

When small talk stalls out, it's often due to a phenomenon we call "mirroring." In our attempts to be polite, we often answer people's questions directly, repeat their observations, or just blandly agree with whatever they say:

James: It's a beautiful day!

John: Yes, it *is* a beautiful day!

By mirroring James's opinion and language, John has followed the social norm, but he's also paralyzed the discussion and made life not worth living. Instead, John needs to practice the *art of disruption* and *move the dialogue forward:*

James: It's a beautiful day!

John: They say that the weather was just like this when the Japanese bombed Pearl Harbor. If that actually happened.

Now James and John are talking! Be provocative. John used his interlocutor's statement as a springboard rather than a reflecting pool. He brought something interesting to the table. It paid off in terms of a drink and deluxe sexual intercourse.

An even better way to break the boring-conversation mirror is to *skip over the expected response, and go somewhere next-level:*

Typical, Boring "Mirroring"	Better
Ron: How was your flight?	**Ron:** How was your flight?
Carlos: My flight was good!	**Carlos:** I'd be more intrigued by an airline where your ticket price was based on your body weight and IQ.
Beverly: It's hot today.	**Beverly:** It's hot today.
Gino: Yeah, it sure is hot.	**Gino:** In this dimension, yes.
Riz: What's up?	**Riz:** What's up?
Keil: Hey, what's up?	**Keil:** Washing your chicken just splatters the bacteria everywhere.

Chapter 3

Parties

MAKE LOVE TO YOUR NIGHTMARE.

CASE STUDY: **Wendy**

Wendy M. was excited to accompany her friend Rhonda to a fundraising cocktail party for the local public library. The theme was "*The Great Gatsby* and Dinosaurs."

Wendy sewed her own brachiosaurus costume out of recycled felt and memorized some facts about sauropods.

"The first sign of trouble was when Rhonda picked me up for the party," Wendy remembers. "Rhonda was dressed as a flapper—and she looked seriously askance at my dinosaur costume."

"It was a *Great Gatsby* party," Rhonda says. "It just doesn't make sense that it would be '*The Great Gatsby and* dinosaurs.' That wasn't what the invitation said."

"Maybe there was a misprint on mine," says Wendy, dejectedly. "Turned out the party was wall-to-wall *jazz people*. I was the only dinosaur. I sulked in the corner, mentally giving everyone the finger."

Then something unexpected happened.

"After about ten minutes, all those Coco Chanel bitches started coming up to me and asking about my costume," Wendy says. "And I had a ton to tell them about brachiosauruses, the Jurassic period, felt crafting, my relationship problems—everything. I made lots of new friends and raised eighty dollars for the library. It turned out to be a great night!"

Parties are the worst. You just stand around like an owl, scared shitless.

It doesn't have to be that way. Wendy's discovery holds a lesson for us all: Difference spawns conversation. Too often, we worry about blending in when what's needed is a dose of disruption. By bringing something different to the party, Wendy gave people an excuse to come strike up a conversation.

Does the principle of disruption mean you should wear huge clown shoes to a ballet recital or face paint to bowling night?

Maybe.

And don't just think of this idea as loosening up the "squares." A Prada suit might go unnoticed at an art auction, but it will get you some attention at a Phish concert.

Nor is disruption just about costumes and props. Wendy thoughtfully supplemented her floppy felt dino getup with some cold, hard facts about the mega-lizard. Bring some *unexpected facts, opinions, and ideas* to the conversation, too. You can also bring a party game. Everyone loves the old favorites: spin the bottle, charades, cornhole. You can supplement these with verbal party games: linguistic first-aid kits at the ready in case of a talk meltdown ...

BONKING

Cyclists and marathon runners talk about "bonking"—in the middle of a race, just when it seems like everything's going great, they hit a wall of low blood sugar. Their legs turn to jelly, their stomach cramps up, and they start braying like donkeys.

The same thing can happen at a party. Things are humming, but then you run out of easy topics. Your mind freezes up, and your mouth starts opening and closing like a fish. Ma ma ma ma ma. To avoid bonking, runners carry simple carbs in their fanny packs. Midrace, they will gobble some honey ham, hummus, or giblets. Protein foods.

So when your conversation is bonking, inject a little "sugar boost." A classic is to suddenly, out of the blue, ask the person to choose between two things, especially things that evoke a visceral ethical or moral choice. Once they choose, they have to defend their choice vigorously.

THE "VERSUS" GAME

* Pie vs. cake

* Snake vs. turtle

* Roe vs. Wade

* Windsurfing vs. hang gliding

* Kramer vs. Kramer

* Caffeine-free vs. gluten-free for the rest of your life

* Immortality vs. guaranteed death at sixty-seven

* Breaking up in person vs. breaking up by phone or text

* Breaking up in person vs. faking own death

* Submarine vs. blimp

* Lion vs. tiger (fight)

* Lion vs. tiger (pet)

* Wrestling vs. sunbathing

* Cash vs. credit card

* Motorcycle vs. scooter

* Wine vs. beer

* Physician-assisted suicide vs. Astronaut Barbie

* Snickers vs. Payday

* You vs. me (leg wrestling)

EXTREME BONKING

Needless to say, levels of bonking vary. Some cases are so severe there's no recovering. Suddenly, you cannot summon a single word of English, cannot even remember your name. Scientists still can't say what, exactly, causes these rare mainframe meltdowns, only that when they happen you look like a beached jellyfish.

What's needed in these instances is the granddaddy of force quits, the fake faint. Hit the ground hard and stay down till someone calls 911. Feel free to "come to" in the ambulance, or ride it out a little longer, just to see where it goes. This whole experience is now a story you can share the next time you feel a "bonk" coming on! Boom. Problem solved. Snake eats its own tail *and becomes even stronger.*

SHY-2-SHY

One reason parties are horrible is because they are filled with shy people. You might even be one of them. Putting shy strangers together in a social setting is like trying to force hermit crabs to play together. It's disgusting.

By definition, shy people are hard to talk to. It's not that they don't have a lot to offer. They just get the shaft in our loudmouth culture, and no one pays attention to them, which they don't seem to mind. Still, if you want to engage a shy, try these strategies:

* Approach at an angle. Direct eye contact, a big smile, and a firm handshake can spook a shy guy or girl. It's like holding up a bowie knife and sprinting straight at a baby deer.

* To begin with, focus the conversation on something in the surrounding area. Above all, do not comment on the shy person or their shyness. You can even mistakenly "see" something ("Oh my god! Is that a spider monkey on that giant cat's muscle car?") to prompt the shy person to correct you and start them talking.

* Don't interrogate. Instead dangle possibilities— think of yourself as an Internet interface with the hope that they'll double-click on one of these statements: "I'm really curious about computer programming . . . and duck hunting . . . and making homemade jam . . . and . . . uh, come on, dude, I'm dyin' here. Tarot cards?"

* Get comfortable with silence. Be like the gathering darkness for the evening primrose and give the shy person space to open up.

* Bond over your (actual or feigned) shared discomfort: "Sorry, I get awkward in social situations. But you seem like you might understand, and I'm sure you've got a lot of interesting things to say."

DINNER PARTY GAMES

Congratulations! Someone invited you over for a meal, either mistakenly or on purpose. But don't celebrate just yet. Careers, marriages, and even science can hinge on what's said between or during bites. Don't just arrive hungry—arrive hungry for *success*. If you want to move past the same old boring biographical hogshit, try these activities, which will guide your conversation into the fecund realm of imaginative exploration. These gambits and contests can be played by the whole party or on the side by two or three conspirators.

* *Movie pitch*. Improvise a movie pitch, starting with a made-up title. To generate a title, open up a book to a random page and read the first two words on the page—that's your title. You can generate the main character by asking one person for their uncle's name and another person for their pet's name, and then combining—such as, "Stephen Red Rocket."

* *Start a Band*. Go around a circle, and use the name of two or more objects you see in the order you see them to make the best indie band name: e.g., Clock Head, Juicer Man, Dog's Butthole Computer. The group then votes on a winner. Bonus points if you can hum a tune or describe your band's first music video to go viral.

* *Dubbing Game*. Extra large party? Pick a couple across the room, out of earshot, and dub their conversation.

* *Information Quest*. Ask a group of people what the annual production of automobiles was in the United States last year. No one will know, so insist that they guess. Ten million? Alex, what do you think? Eight million? Tanya, you say thirty million? Any other guesses? Pause dramatically before you reveal the answer, and then say, "Actually, I have no idea." Then discuss how you might construct an answer based on only the things you *do* know. No Googling.

* *Two Lies and Two Lies*. Tell four lies about yourself.

Chapter 4

Drive-By Conversations

PERFECTING THE PASSING EXCHANGE.

Every day we intersect with strangers and semi-strangers for minutes or even seconds at a time. Bagel guy. Bank teller. Tollbooth girl. Bank teller again (left your bagel there).

If you're like most people, and most people are, you probably sleepwalk through these glancing exchanges, saving yourself for the "real" conversations. But guess what? Yeah, exactly. We don't even need to say it. So how about treating these interactions as the huge opportunities they are, akin to space exploration in the 1960s? We've (allegedly) conquered the moon. Now it's time to conquer the men and women we see every day. These are real conversations; this is your real life. Pee first and suit up!

WHAT TO TALK ABOUT
WITH THE MAIL
CARRIER

What's the angriest or happiest you've ever seen anyone with regard to mail?

What's the best/worst mail scene depicted in the movies?

What's the stupidest/coolest mailbox you've ever seen?

What's the freakiest sex toy that you've ever imagined was inside a box that you delivered?

Do you ever wear the blue shorts on your day off?

Your calf muscles represent what exactly?

Sleet? Come on.

Thoughts on stamp collectors?

How come pornos never feature the mailman, only the UPS guy and the pizza guy?

WHAT TO TALK
ABOUT WITH THE UPS
DELIVERY PERSON

Softball match with FedEx. Lotta people would pay to see that, right?

What part of your body is sorest?

What makes you cross?

What's preferable—carrying a back-breakingly huge package or a humiliatingly small one?

What's the strangest package-delivery-related injury you've ever experienced or heard of?

The mailman says you guys are lightweights.

Do you ever wear the brown shorts on your day off?

Have you ever fallen out of the truck?

Seriously, how much time could you possibly save by not having a door?

Do you send most of your sex toys through UPS?

WHAT TO TALK ABOUT WITH THE GROCERY CHECKER

What's the angriest or happiest you've ever seen anyone while paying for their groceries?

What's the ratio of people who make eye contact versus those who won't look at you?

What's the most coveted job in the store (besides checker)?

What's the process for getting to play with the sprayer in produce?

Do you ever count how much cash passes through your hands in a single day?

When fantasies of stealing it pop into your head, what movie star do you imagine running away with?

What would you guys talk about?

How do you wash a conveyor belt?

Did you have any dreams last night?

Are all humans liars?

WHAT TO TALK ABOUT
WITH THE BUTCHER

What's "tri tip"?

How is a meat saw different than a regular saw for sawing flesh?

What's the strangest request you've ever had for a type of meat or a type of cut?

How often do you Google meat-related stuff?

Ever seen a real flying fish? I have.

How come no one's made cows lift weights? Bigger steaks!

When you watch horror movies, do you ever think: I could do that better?

What meat is best for double entendres: beef, pork, or bone-in chicken breasts?

WHAT TO TALK ABOUT WITH THE TOLLBOOTH OPERATOR

Is there a God?

WHAT TO TALK ABOUT WITH THE CABLE GUY

What kind of setup do you have at your own condo?

What's the worst hoarder situation you've ever seen in someone's home?

What are the most televisions you've seen in someone's house? The biggest TV?

What do you think you would've done, career-wise, if nobody had invented television?

Did you see that movie with Jim Carrey? I forget what it's called, but he plays a cable guy.

Is there a maximum number of shows that can fit through a single cable? Do you worry about those really long shows? What about the thick ones?

Why can't you arrive at a specific time? Even plumbers can arrive at a specific time.

WHAT TO TALK ABOUT WITH THE PLUMBER

F*#$@n' cable guys, amirite?

WHAT TO TALK ABOUT WITH YOUR DOCTOR

What's it like for you when *you* go to the doctor? Hard to set aside the judgment?

Are older doctors smarter because they have more experience—or scarier because their knowledge is outdated?

What has been your funniest "blooper" while practicing medicine?

Have you ever seen the movie *Being John Malkovich*?

Do you want me to take my clothes off now?

What about now?

The knee bone is connected to the—which is it again?

With your talent, you could've done anything, yet you became a surgeon—why?

Is there a God?

WHAT TO TALK ABOUT WITH THE METER MAID OR METER "MISTER"

You f#cking *saw* me running.

I was getting f#ckin' change!

Sixty bucks!? F########CK!

WHAT TO TALK
ABOUT WITH THE
BANK TELLER

What's the most valuable thing you've ever seen in a safety deposit box?

Which box is it in?

Any rules about what I can put in there? Wet bathing suit okay?

Are you wearing pants with an elastic waistband?

Do you ever just "not bother" from the waist down?

I'm not going to hold up this bank [wink].

Do you ever go in the vault and just smell the money?

Ever punched someone in the face?

How often do you reach for the alarm bu—you're reaching right now, aren't you?

Coffee?

WHAT TO TALK ABOUT
WITH THE TAXI DRIVER

What's the biggest fare you've ever had?

What's the strangest object someone has transported in your cab?

Where are you from and don't take that in any way except that I'm interested in the world.

What's the craziest thing that's happened in this cab?

What's the craziest nonsexual thing that's happened in this cab?

Lotta pizza guys in pornos. Not so many cab drivers.

Show me your laugh when someone tries to pay with a Diners Club card.

What are you running from, emotionally?

WHAT TO TALK ABOUT
WITH YOUR DENTIST

You know the drill. It's in your mouth. And your chatty dentist is peppering you with questions. You've got to turn the tables early on, before your pie-hole is stuffed. Front-load the interaction with questions designed to elicit long answers.

> What made you want to become a dentist?

> How has dentistry changed since you entered the profession?

> What's the grossest thing someone's hidden in their gums? The most expensive?

> What do you think about orthodontists? Don't hold back.

Then, as your dentist works, fill any conversational "cavity" by flashing a few preprepared index cards:

Yes, of course I floss daily.

I can't hear you over the voice in my fillings.

By "daily" I mean, you know, "monthly."

Pirate radio is real.

Ha ha ha! That's really funny.

I come from a long line of miners.

yes.

No.

TOTALLY, that reminds me of Being John Malkovich.

WHAT TO TALK ABOUT
IN CLOSE QUARTERS

Some say the average American spends a total of six months stuck in broken elevators over the course of a lifetime. Is this true? Relax your sphincter. The point is, some of our greatest conversational successes arise from situations in which exit is not an option. Whether you're marooned on a ski lift or waiting with your three-legged race partner for the starting gun to fire, forced intimacy is undeniably awkward—but it's also an opportunity to push through to another level. So get off your toadstool and take it to the Thunderdome.

Clip and save these surefire prompts for the next time you're locked in a talk box with no way out:

DILEMMAS, DILEMMAS, DILEMMAS

If your partner were having an affair, would you rather know or never find out?

Would you starve a rattlesnake to death for ten dollars? What about a rabbit? (Continue up the evolutionary chain until you get to *Australopithecus afarensis*. Always stop there. Don't go "late hominid.")

Would you scratch a kid's arm for a free pair of Armani sunglasses?

Which of your relatives would you rather see swallowed by a sinkhole? Why?

What's the biggest regret of your life?

If we ever get out of this, will you marry me? Would you marry my brother? He's amazing.

How tall do you think the Devil was? Are you just guessing or have you met him?

CULTURAL CONNECTIONS

First concert you ever went to?

Favorite candy/cereal/board game as a kid?

How are you different from the others in your family/hometown/nation of birth?

In what ways are you exactly like them?

Classiest font?

Would you rather make love to C-3PO or R2-D2?

PRACTICAL CONSIDERATIONS

Do you know how to fix a broken elevator?

Tipping While Talking: The Food-Delivery Person

Talking to restaurant delivery people while carefully calculating their tip can run even the nimblest minds aground. Grandmaster Garry Kasparov could reportedly play eighteen games of chess simultaneously—and win them all—but when the pizza guy showed up he'd collapse in the corner, cross-eyed and rigid, just to avoid the tip calculation.

Use this simple guide next time you order food, and free yourself up to have a brief, pleasant exchange with the fellow human who delivers it.

First, calculate your baseline tip immediately after ordering, and before getting caught back up in whatever made you too lazy to cook in the first place. Baseline = 10 percent of the final bill.

Before tax? No. *After* tax. Jesus, listen to yourself.

Then, when the food arrives, answer the door warmly, but don't exhaust the person. The average delivery person has to make eleven deliveries per shift, and half of those deliveries include sex. Not as much as the UPS guy, but still.

Finally, based on your exchange at the door, adjust the baseline tip. You're in the trenches now—time to stuff all those nebulous moral and aesthetic calculations into your mind blender and produce a smoothie of fairness and reason. Use this handy key to adjust your tip appropriately:

- Are they nice? +1 dollar

- Are they older than fifty? +1 dollar

- Food spillage? –1 dollar

- Raining/snowing? +1 dollar

- Genuine smile? +1 dollar

- Frightening smile? +1 dollar (They have your address)

- Fancy car? –1 dollar

- Incredibly fancy car? +1 dollar for being super rich and doing what they love, food delivery

- Popped collar? –1 dollar

- Popped collar bone? +1 dollar

- Friendly interaction with your kids or pet? –1 dollar for pandering

- Do they deliver food for a living? +1 dollar

Chapter 5

Friends

PUT A ROCKET ON YOUR TANDEM GO-KART.

CASE STUDY: **Jarolyn and Pam**

Jarolyn R. and Pam F. were college roommates who became lifelong friends after the remarkable realization that both were adopted, and after Pam forgave Jarolyn for lying about being adopted. They would bare their souls late into the night, pushing exciting conversational boundaries. But over the years, the friendship slackened. Now they mostly exchange updates about their kids, and sometimes Jarolyn slips back into the adoption thing. They are in a classic rut, and not the fun kind.

How are old friends supposed to keep having fresh, stimulating exchanges? In the movies, true friendship is a sacred and dynamic sphere where deeply bonded intimates say whatever's on their minds and nudge each other into better versions of themselves. In real life, there's nothing on our minds; we're busy and our inferior selves will do. We circle endlessly around the same topics, offer the same advice, eat the same old apple. Your job as a true friend is to find a way to stay fresh.

Tip One: Switch out your culture inputs. Do you normally watch nature documentaries? Watch some Turkish sci-fi films instead. Do you normally listen to podcasts on your commute? Listen for a week to whatever your grandmother's favorite music was in 1954. Do you normally read *The Economist*? You're lying.

Tip Two: Next time you plan to meet a friend, get to the meeting place a half hour early and just start walking. You can walk a two-mile loop in thirty minutes. No technology allowed. No straining for interesting thoughts, either. Just walk quietly. Through the miracle of science, the extra blood pumping through your capillaries will enlarge the mental molecules in your frontal lobe, before replicating into your thorax. It sounds intense, but it just might be the thing you need to discover surprises in your brainpan.

BREAK THE TABOO: TALK ABOUT MONEY

CASE STUDY: **Steve, Gwen, Steve, Michiko**

Steve L., Gwen G., Steve S., and Michiko M. went out for a drink after their twentieth high school reunion. They were okay talking about the old days, mutual friends, family life, and so on. *But when talk got near the subject of money, an uncomfortable silence arose.*

Steve L. was loaded (on daiquiris and on family inheritance), and Steve S. was struggling financially (due to stupid career choices and a curse that a motorcycle goblin had put on him in Hawai'i). Gwen and Michiko were somewhere in between: doing okay, money-wise, but not without worries. The four old friends regarded one another and their finances warily. Did Steve L. have an obligation to help Steve S. out with a loan? Why had Steve S. bought a pit bull if he could barely feed himself? Should Gwen give up work to raise a child? How come Michiko ordered a pinot grigio that cost *twelve dollars* ($12) a glass? And who was going to pick up the tab?

Money brings up many, many uncomfortable feelings between friends, such as guilt, jealousy, and . . . those two, mainly. But what if we could somehow transcend all that? What if we could not just stop avoiding the subject, but wade *into* it? We're all thinking about money; it's a relief to put those thoughts on the table and be honest about our deepest financial fears and fantasies.

With a longtime friend, take turns reading aloud each of the questions below. Answer one another with complete honesty. Stop the exercise if while doing this the two of you threaten to break up the friendship, form a business partnership, have sex, or all three at once.

How much money do you have in your combined checking and savings accounts right now?

How much did you pay for your house? Or, how much is your monthly rent?

Did you get an allowance as a kid? Did that help or hurt your relationship to money?

How much do you think your own life is worth? (Subtract $25K if your answer is "You can't put a price on life.")

Talk about a time you got ripped off.

Talk about a time you ripped someone off.

Do you feel you *deserve* a certain amount of money?

Ever paid someone for sex, directly or indirectly? What do you mean "indirectly"?

If you have any paper currency in your pocket, rip a bill in half now. If you cannot bring yourself to do this, why not? If you can, explain yourself.

What single expenditure do you regret the most?

EMOTIONAL FRACKING

With hydraulic fracturing, deep fissures in rocks are created by injecting fluid into narrow cracks in order to release natural gas and petroleum. The scientific community largely opposes "fracking" because of groundwater contamination and blah blah blah. We at *What to Talk About* endorse the procedure—when it's *emotions* you're fracking.

Having built up your foundation of comfort and trust using the previous tools in this book, you're now ready for deep probing. Remember: The goal of talking isn't merely to pass the time. At its most triumphant, conversation is Balboa discovering the Pacific, Franklin discovering the wooden tooth. Do it right, and you'll frack open virgin bedrock in yourself and others, yielding untold emotional insight and wealth. Might that be unsettling and thrilling? You know the fracking answer.

Sit face-to-face with your conversational partner and just go at it with these prompts, no mercy:

> Describe yourself in ten words.
>
> How would different family members describe you?
>
> What about your friends? Your coworkers? Whose description do you like the most?
>
> Are you improving with age or worsening?

Which areas are more dry/moist than they used to be?

How are you most misunderstood by the world?

What do you most misunderstand about yourself?

What do you really want that no one knows?

Describe yourself in one word.

CONVERSATION IN EXTREMIS: GETTING BACK IN TOUCH

In this era of bulging in-boxes, unrequited voicemail messages, and social media updates, actual talking gets neglected. Between friends, nothing is worse than silence, particularly when that silence extends for weeks, months, years. Owing a friend a phone call or email makes for a horrible stew of guilt and resentment, a stew that mushrooms and stinks the longer you wait. In other words, it's hard to talk when the main thing you want to talk about (or apologize for) is that you haven't been talking. Thankfully, there's a three-step process for finding your way out:

1. Stop reading this book. Your old roommate had a baby eight months ago, and you still haven't wished him congratulations? Quit dithering and get out the stationery. The real stuff. Hard copy. You didn't really think there'd be a solution that didn't involve getting back in touch, did you? What, like faking your own death? Far too much hassle—remember, you couldn't even write a simple email!

2. Begin with a heartfelt apology. You might be tempted to blame your silence on some concocted illness. Yes, do that—you did bad and you need a big play here. But resist the temptation to make too much of your excuse. The person will know it's bogus, anyway.

3. Move on, so your transgression doesn't define your relationship from here on out. Schedule a visit promptly, take your friend out to a steak dinner, and pick up where you left off pre-diss. Note: If you're still getting signals he or she intends to stay mad indefinitely, apologize again, and go out to get a special apology gift from your car. Except, your gift is driving away super fast.

Chapter 6

Mapping Your Personal Style

ARE YOU A PANCAKE? OR ARE YOU A STEAMROLLER?

CONVERSATIONAL styles fall on a spectrum. At the extremes of the spectrum are opposite types: Steamrollers and Pancakes.

Each style has positive and negative aspects, and each can squash or enliven a conversation. The most important thing is to identify your own type and then, with that self-awareness, use your strengths—and develop your weaknesses—for the good of humanity.

Like their highway-flattening namesake, Steamrollers love to talk. At their best, they can salvage a silent stare-fest by filling in the awkward talk-crevasses and laying a sturdy base. Then everyone can get across and reach the conversational peak without falling into ice-blue canyons. At their worst, Steamrollers insist on having the first and last words, and most of the middle ones.

Pancakes instinctively avoid talking. They are adept at deflecting direct inquiries, nodding mutely, and at their best, posing provocative questions that give others space to ripen like strawberries on a short stack. At their worst, Pancakes become invisible. They swallow opinions and ideas that would have helped move the conversation forward.

To develop your skills as a conversationalist, you must put time into developing your conversational alter ego. Steamrollers should practice listening while stuffing their mouths with keys or ice chips.

Shy Pancakes: Start by making your physical presence known to the Steamrollers in a nonchallenging, nonconfrontational way. Wear your red boots to the party, and point one toe into the conversation circle. Then try dangling a conversation piñata (see page 155). You don't need to launch into a full-fledged soliloquy, but timing your responses, and increasing the time with each answer, is a good way to stretch yourself.

With this in mind, you're ready to take this book's Quick Quonversation Quiz™ to see where you fall on the spectrum:

QUICK QUONVERSATION QUIZ™

1 When I'm at a funeral, I:

    A. know just what to say to comfort the bereaved, but am afraid to say it.

    B. can't remember any stories about the dead person.

    C. tell jokes that people misinterpret as racist.

    D. do gymnastics until the hostess asks me to leave.

2 When I am in a conversation with someone smarter or more interesting than myself, I:

    A. try to do more listening than talking.

    B. worry I'll say something stupid.

    C. fancy-whistle Broadway show tunes until it's my turn to talk.

    D. It is impossible that I would ever meet such a person.

3 When expressing my opinion, I:

    A. cinch my hoodie over my face.

    B. am always alone on a Ferris wheel.

    C. am always 110 percent right.

    D. deserve another shot of Jäger as a reward for bequeathing my genius to the common people.

4 The topic I am most comfortable discussing is:

A. politics.

B. sports.

C. my dissertations.

D. the smell of my sports trophies.

5 The romantic comedy star I identify most with is:

A. Jennifer Aniston.

B. Paul Rudd.

C. Steve Buscemi.

D. Trash-Compactor Squid.

Score yourself:

Mark 1 point for each A, 2 points for each B, 3 points for each C, and 4 points for each D. Total your points and refer to the following chart:

18–20: Seek help. You possibly exhibit narcissistic personality disorder.

15–17: Classic "Steamroller." You need to listen more.

11–14: Versatile ambivert. You know when to listen and when to talk. Keep up the good work, but don't get cocky.

8–10: You err on the side of keeping your thoughts to yourself. Push yourself; get off your Quiet Diet™.

5–7: You're a Pancake, and you're getting flattened by Steamrollers. The world needs you to rise up.

THE NEXT-LEVEL LEVEL

Let's say you're doing great: You're listening when others are speaking, and then talking like a pro about animals, sports, feelings, Sailor Jerry (see page 153). It couldn't be going better. Or could it?

For conversationalists keen to push themselves to the next level, we recommend an unorthodox step: *the check-in*. For self-identified Steamrollers, in the middle of your next monologue, stop and ask, "Are you with me?" or "What do *you* think?" Make sure you haven't "lost the plot" or your audience. Note that nodding, blinking, or sneezing by others is not necessarily a sign of comprehension; insist on a verbal response. Checking in is also simply polite on your part. If you are a self-identified Pancake, make sure the other person isn't talking in order to paper over your silence. Ask, "May I interject something?" Then interject something. A conversation is a heavy burden when it's carried alone.

Overachievers will prefer a more robust check-in. Hand out the scorecard below after your next exchange with a friend, coworker, or bank teller. Remember: The quest for self-betterment—and milking each interaction for the most amount of milk—is something everyone appreciates.

 ## THE CHECK-IN

Nice talking with you! How could our conversation have been improved?

Please rate me on a scale of 1 to 10 in the following categories (in which 1 = way too little, 10 = way too much):

___ Active listening
___ Bullshit

___ Yawning
___ Lively debate

___ Eye contact
___ Emotional probing

___ Flirting
___ Actual probing

___ Facts and relevant information
___ Texting/checking iPhone

___ Shredded pork in teeth

What additional topics should I have touched on?

(circle one)

Family   Science

Hobbies   The fleetingness of it all

The roots of your   The weather
happiness/unhappiness

I am ...

(circle one)

Clever   Not clever

Somewhat clever   A Steamroller/Pancake

Chapter 7

Family

HARNESS YOUR NUCLEAR POWER.

Dad: Volvos used to be a lot boxier, didn't they? Now look at them. What was wrong with boxy? Why does everything have to be like everything else? It's assimilation is what it is.

Son: I can't believe I used to live in your testicle.

If talking with your family brings out your inner fifteen-year-old, or if you're actually fifteen and talking with your family is, like, aggravating that fact, it's time to look at the problem in a new light. When chitchat between strangers suffers, it's often from a lack of familiarity. When we don't know anything about one another, it's hard to find a conversational foothold. Within families, however, the opposite is true: We know far, far too much, and achieving closeness is not the problem. Our intimacy prevents us from finding a safe distance.

FICTIONALIZE THEM

Your family is crazy, batshit loco. But you can still learn to tolerate—even enjoy—talking with them without so much as an hour of therapy. You just need a good plot.

H-h-huh? The trick is to see them not as relatives but as characters in a book or movie. When you imagine your family as the cast of a screwball comedy or a trippy David Lynch movie, their antics stop being irritating and start becoming fascinating.

1. Identify the genre. Romance? Drama? Dark Scandinavian thriller? Figure out what section of the book or video store carries your family saga, and you're that much closer to finding out what to say to these people.

2. Who plays what part, and what's their motivation? Once you determine what drives your dad to feed bacon grease to the hamster, his erratic behavior will start to make a certain twisted narrative sense.

3. Remind yourself, as often as necessary, that these people are *not real* and are *not related to you*. Talk to them as if they are fictional characters come to life. Ask about their earliest memories. Inquire about the hardest parts of their day. Take lots of notes. Remember: You've got some of fiction's most original, vivid

characters sitting at your *own dinner table*.
Now's your chance to ask them anything you'd
ever want to know.

4. Type it up, sell it. With a good agent and foreign
   rights, you should earn enough to acquire a
   new family.

THANKSGIVING

When it comes to talking with your family, it doesn't get
much worse than the holidays. A misunderstanding here,
an unearthed grudge there, and before you know it, Uncle
Saul gets a Chianti goblet in the ramus.

Unlike the family drama exercise we've recommended
above, our Thanksgiving strategy is to gather real information. Pretend you're a private investigator, and your job is
to collect facts from as many different family members as
possible. Rather than being part of this mess, you're looking at it from the outside in.

Start with a piece of disputed history: Choose something in
the safely distant past. Childhood family myths are a good
place to start: Did Dad really throw a poison dart at his math
teacher? Interview aunts, uncles, grandparents. Interview
the younger generation, even though they weren't born
when the incident occurred. Ask them to weigh in on Dad's
character. Could he have done such a thing? Get to the bot-

tom of the story. If anyone tries to turn the tables and interview you, chuckle and ask a nephew to fetch your Camels.

Here are the rules:

1. You are only allowed to ask questions. Offer no statements and no opinions.

2. You must write everything down on a notepad. This signals to everyone (including yourself) that you mean business.

Putting yourself in the interviewer role—and giving yourself a job—will change your whole holiday experience. The conversation becomes not about you, and you'll be giving a gift to the party (see the "Parties" chapter, page 33) in the form of a real conversation topic, where everyone's opinion is listened to and recorded.

The private-investigator conceit will work for most family gatherings, but you should also come prepared with some additional tools for talking with three subspecies of family members: very young people, very old people, and teenagers. Every family has them, and they require special conversational tactics. Children might have small minds, but they frequently pose adult-size challenges in conversation. What words do they understand? What are they capable of discussing? Do you get credit for talking to them if their parents aren't around? The elderly, meanwhile, present another set of hurdles. What are their interests? Are they sad about being old, or into it? Teens, for their part, are like Rubik's Cubes: a fun challenge for four or five minutes, but ultimately a waste of money. Following, some helpful prompts . . .

FOR CHILDREN EIGHT AND UNDER

What do you think your parents talk about when you're not around?

Do an impression of them. Do you know what an impression is? What about a toupée? Or seltzer?

Regrets so far?

What are your plans if you never grow any taller?

Animals you'd be comfortable riding into battle?

What if a policeman did a poo-poo on a fire truck?

Little Shy Guys and Gals

Even super-shy little nieces or nephews can usually tell you their age. It's a good warm-up exchange, and of course you'll feign astonishment when they blurt out "five." The flipside? They get asked this fifty times a day, followed by what grade they're in.

If you'd like to connect more meaningfully, try moving into new territory. Ask for their opinion with a simple "would you rather" game, making the choices connect to their lives: "Would you rather be an astronaut or a zookeeper?" "Would you rather have toes made of jelly beans or chocolate eyelashes?"

Take the opinion game to the next level by treating them like a real peer. Ask a multiple-choice conundrum that you need their help with, letting them venture an opinion about you, rather than having them explain themselves. For example: "I was thinking of getting a new purse—do you think it should be green or orange?" Continue in this vein until Mom lets them use her iPad.

FOR TEENAGERS

What kind of bullshit have they got you doing at school?

Who is the most amazing person?

You're breaking out of your pupa, kid. What do you like and dislike about the changes going on inside?

What is your best idea that nobody is hearing?

I'm going to ask if you've heard of Gandhi, and I
just want you to say yes, okay?

If you had to ask for a hundred dollars, which
parent would you ask?

Do an impression of the parent you wouldn't ask.

Wait, did you already steal the money?

If there were nothing holding you back, what
would you like to be doing in ten years?

How big a threat do you think North Korea
represents to the United States right now?
(Respect their intelligence; they may be more
informed than you.)

Who were you texting with this whole time?

FOR ADULTS EIGHTY AND OLDER

Most memorable century?

Least memorable?

Do old people think Florida is crazy, too, or are
they too close to the situation?

Sex during the Eisenhower administration:
Similar? Dos/don'ts?

Best friend ever. Worst enemy ever. Who do you think about more?

You and me, right now: Let's design a nonhorrible nursing home. Just bang it out, be done by 4:30, and grab some dinner.

How much did a _____ cost when you were a kid? (Kidding. Answer's always a nickel.)

Biggest thing you changed your mind about in life?

SKYPING WITH YOUR PARENTS

If you live away from home, and your parents have mastered email, sooner or later they're going to catch wind of the fact that people can now "do a video chat on the computer." When they ask if they can do that with you, here's what to say:

"No."

If they persist, say, "Seriously, no. That's not technically possible. Maybe in the future, but it's still a long way off."

If they keep insisting that it's possible, you may have to admit that it is and agree to a test run on Skype or iChat. But make sure you prepare first:

Next time you visit your parents (but before your first video chat), write their computer password with a Sharpie on their refrigerator door.

A few weeks later, when it comes time to set up the actual video chat, your parents will ask you what their password is. Tell them, "It's on the fridge."

If they say, "It just says 'password,'" tell them that their password—and almost everyone else's password—is actually "password."

Each time you "do a Skype," they're going to see you appear on their screen, and then they'll ask if you can see them.

Say, "No. You have to hit the 'Video' button."

They'll say, "Where is the 'Video' button?"

Plan ahead for this, too. During the same visit where you write their password on the fridge, secretly open Skype on their laptop, find the video button, and circle it on their screen using the Sharpie. There will be a permanent circle on their screen, but just tell them it's a "Google." Hopefully their Skype window will open in the same location, and you can direct them to the circled Video icon. Your mom will likely try to wipe off the Sharpie circle with her finger. Your dad will look at her.

Say, "Mom. Can we just . . . ?"

Now for the actual content of the video chat. They'll likely start with, "It's so clear/fuzzy," and then get distracted looking at themselves talking in the bottom right of their screen. You should slowly move in a side-to-side motion, so they don't say, "Are you there? Did he freeze up, Dick?" Then you'll talk at the same time, and you'll both say, "What?" and your dad will start staring again.

There is no way to say good-bye while video chatting. When you're ready for the call to end, make your dog stand up on his hind legs and do a brief dance for the webcam. Everyone will laugh. Then have the dog accidentally push his nose onto the "Close" button.

Chapter 8

Travel

YOU ARE TO SPEAK HAPPY OTHER COUNTRY
HELLO.

CASE STUDY: **Litia**

Litia B. is an expert traveler. She has climbed Mount Kilimanjaro and watched the sunrise from a glacier in Iceland. She has gone swimming with baby seals in New Zealand, clubbed them in Canada, and been to a club where Seal was playing in Cannes. But whenever she meets folks on the road, all her interesting thoughts and experiences vanish.

"I don't know what's wrong with me," she says. "I meet someone, and suddenly all I can talk about is how annoying American tourists are and how gorgeous the scenery is. What's the point?"

For all those guidebooks explaining what to *do* in exotic locales, few explain what to *say*. We travel to broaden our sense of what's possible—not just in the world but within ourselves. Nevertheless, we often respond to the most sublime experiences on the road with the most awful banalities.

Disoriented, far from home, probably drugged, we snap like rubber bands to the nearest set of platitudes: *This market is so vibrant. This village is so quaint. Why can't life be like this back in the States? Chinese Slim Jims taste soapier.*

Platitudes defeat travel. Received wisdom builds up on our souls like plaque; we leave home to scrape *through* it, not to accumulate more. The trick to changing your travel conversations? Change how you travel.

Here's what to do: The next time you're in, say, Lima, do not attempt to see all of Lima. Don't even see much of Lima. Focus on a single neighborhood and bring along a real, everyday mission. Need a new reed for your clarinet? Ask someone where the nearest music store is. Are you nuts about George Eliot? Hunt down the best old bookstore. Do you collect buttons? That's silly!

Stop an everyday person on the street or in a shop and ask for help.

> **You:** Excuse me, could you tell me where the closest wig store is?
>
> **Sweaty guy at Nokia store:** Wig? What is?
>
> **You:** A wig—you know, like *hair* [pantomime hair].
>
> **S.G.A.N.S:** Wig! Okay. Don't know. But cousin know. Go to frame shop, next block.

And so on. Go to the frame shop, where the cousin behind the counter sends you to his peasant grandmother with the claw hand; she mentions that she grew up in that very building, you ask about life in the old days, and she starts talking about the Fascists—play your cards right and you've got an awesome dinner invite. "Macañaño. It's like . . . how you say? Eh, pasta made from bird shit." Eat it. Unforgettable night, unforgettable conversations.

CHAMELEON CONVERSATION

Another way to expand your conversational possibilities while traveling: Pretend to be someone else for a few days. Adopting a new identity can open up loads of new conversational possibilities.

Try out one of these personas for a (temporary) new you:

THE LOTHARIO/LOTHARIA

Persona: Sex god/dess

Trademarks: Motorcycle with two helmets. Body butter.

Power move: Back rub in the Sacred Springs; crying.

Sample line: "Let's get lost together."

THE HELPLESS WAIF

Persona: Lost, vulnerable; an innocent abroad.

Trademarks: Can't figure out how to book a simple hotel room.

Power move: Actually knows how to book a hotel room.

Sample line: "How much are these weird coins worth? Enough for bus fare? Are those long things buses?"

THE DRIFTING SAGE

Persona: Humble and soulful.

Trademarks: Spiritual know-it-all-ism; salami breath.

Power move: You just bought him/her dinner.

Sample line: "You already know the answer in your heart."

URINE BIG TROUBLE

Your trip has been a wild success. You remembered tons of high school French, found a sweet wig shop, and made out with a security guard in the Louvre.

But suddenly you find yourself at a restaurant bathroom, standing at a urinal next to a stranger.

Como se dice "awkward"? Thirty seconds of excruciating silence, and a week's worth of conversational triumphs go down the drain.

Worse yet: Your urinal mate is a fellow countryman. If conversation does arise, it's almost guaranteed to lapse into obvious statements about how different this place is from your shared home.

Don't throw in the towel just yet. Cut him off at the pass. Small talk, endorsed elsewhere in this book, is the wrong medicine here. What you need is a head shot. Guard down, outside of his home turf, he's more likely to go along for the ride:

> Quick, let's each confess a sin on the count of three.

> Tell me one thing you're proud of. Go!

Is this the life you imagined for yourself?

If that cake were an edible cake, which kind of cake would you want it to be?

This won't always work, but when it does, your pee-mate's initial surprise will quickly turn to delight, and the uncomfortable silence to a brief but profound interaction. Anyway, you've got nothing to lose. Except a bladderful of urine.

Note: Are you a woman at a urinal? Common mistake— don't beat yourself up. Just retrace your steps and look for the room full of other women. Enter a stall, where anonymity facilitates big-picture musings:

Anyone want to talk, or should this just be me time?

How does WiFi work?

Don't hover and spray. We're better than that!

Banned Conversations

These overused travel-talk gambits have simply expired. Sorry.

- Faux-amazement at local cuisine
- Faux-shame over cuisine back home
- "Teach me to say something dirty in your language!"
- "People are so friendly here!"
- Joking about accents*

* Except Irish.

Chapter 9

Romance

DATE AND MATE LIKE A BOSS.

CASE STUDY: **Leroy**

Leroy W., a forty-nine-year-old third base coach, was in the cereal aisle; Monica M., a fifty-one-year-old cellist, was in produce. By his own calculations, Leroy had no more than two minutes before Monica would reach the checkout lane and be out of his life forever. He had one shot.

"Excuse me," he said, amping up his confidence. "I was wondering, don't you think it's weird that you never hear about ghosts appearing at the *gym?*"

"I do hear about it," she said. Remarkably, Monica runs a respected listserv on the subject. "I need to go, sorry."

Leroy was crestfallen, and sort of surly, too.

"I don't get it," he told us later. "I was quoting from your book, assholes."

Leroy is tall and decent-looking, with obvious intelligence, symmetrical features, and a full twelve fingers. How did he bungle such a basic conversation?

He didn't—Leroy bungled a conversation that's a thousand miles from basic. Romance exists in a category all its own, in a separate country from other conversational protocol, surrounded by a forbidding moat of diarrhea. All the rules so far about what to talk about? Out the window when it comes to romance. Out the window and, incredibly, right into the moat.

The trick to a successful romantic introduction is to stop thinking there's a trick. Don't be clever. Don't be interesting. Don't be elaborate. Dig down, find one honest bone buried in that heaving slop of nerves and misplaced swagger.

We helped Leroy uncover his honest bone and had him camp out in produce until Monica shopped again. When she did, this is what he said:

"Hey. I hope this isn't too weird—I know we don't know each other, and just the other day I blew it trying to start a conversation, but you look smart and pretty and funny, and I just had this feeling you'd be super fun to talk with. I'm going to tuck my email address into your oranges here, and if you want to grab some coffee or something one day, then give a shout. I'm Leroy, by the way. And I'm feeling 85 percent self-conscious about this now, so I'm going to hide in the cheese aisle until you're gone. Bye!"

Two weeks later, Leroy and Monica had five children and nine grandchildren.

WHAT TO TALK ABOUT
WITH CRUSHES

You've done it again. You've gone and developed a crush on someone in the service industry. But here's the problem: If you screw up this romantic overture, you can never enter that coffeehouse/doctor's office/shrimp house again. So, instead of going the honesty route, gently test the waters with specially designed romantic small talk that has plausible deniability built in.

WHAT *NOT* TO SAY TO THE HOT BARISTA AT GROUNDZ FOR DISMISSAL

Cleverness is seldom clever.

What Not to Say	Why Not
"I read on Wikipedia that the main variables in a shot of espresso are *size* and *length* [wink]."	You're attempting a *double entendre*, but that's way long, long . . . deeply hard . . . See? We can't do it well, either.
"Been running my home machine at 205, hot for a single-origin bean, brings out the fru . . . whoa, is *that* the new Aeropress?"	She sees Comic-Con in her future, with a side of model railroading.

"If I had a racehorse, I'd name him after you: Seabiscuit! That's your name, right?"

Just ask her name.

"Do you want to go out for coffee sometime?"

Look around. Would you invite the Cinnabon girl out for a cinnamon roll? You would? Good for you. Ballsy. You don't need this book.

WHAT TO SAY TO THE CUTE BIKE MECHANIC AT CYCLE KILLER

Successful flirtatious small talk creates an opening for a connection without presuming one, allowing both people to sidestep if the desire isn't reciprocated.

What to Say	Why
"I don't see how anyone in their right mind could prefer cake to pie."	You're hoping for an "Oh my god, me too" reaction.
"Can I smell your hair?"	Everyone likes to have their hair smelled.
"Can you break a McKinley?"	McKinley is on the five-hundred-dollar bill. If he doesn't know this, he's not sophisticated enough for you. If he does, he's impressed!
"That's a cool shirt—it helps make your arms look the right length."	The hook is set: He is thinking, "If I have to, I will spend my whole life proving to her that my arms are long enough."

THE FIRST DATE:
A FOUR-PART MASTER
CLASS

Once your romantic target accepts your initial entreaty, your conversational challenges begin in earnest. Here is our one-part class in first-date success, broken conveniently into four parts.

THE BEGINNER CLASS

Stop talking about yourself. Ask the other person about him- or herself.

So simple. And yet so difficult. But if you can follow this cardinal rule, you will get so much more _____.*

* Fill in the blank with whatever you want to get more of, even lowly respect; you're the captain of your own -%^!.

INTERMEDIATE FAQ

QUESTION 1: What if both people on the first date are following the beginner's cardinal rule? Won't we just circle around on an Interrogative Merry-Go-Round?

ANSWER: Yes, that's the idea. Answer the question, but keep circling back. For example: "...so that's how I fell in love with scuba diving. Have you ever looked at dugong and felt they had a soul?"

The idea is that you share yourself, but don't hog the spotlight. Keep connecting back to your date.

QUESTION 2: What if I'm stuck on a date with a Steamroller (see page 69) who loves talking about him- or herself and has forgotten there's another person present?

ANSWER: You have two strategies:

> Strategy A: Look at your phone and say, "I have Chlamydia. It's also called the Clap!"
>
> Strategy B: Use an "honesty interruption." Say: "You might not realize it, but you've been talking about yourself for [look at watch] seven minutes straight. I want to give you some feedback: If you're hoping to get some of this [point to your head and/or zones of interest], you're sabotaging yourself. I also want to give you the benefit of the doubt, since you may be nervous. Let's aim for more of a dialogue."

With Strategy B, you're giving the other person a gift. Depending on the response, go back to Chlamydia.

ADVANCED ALTERNATIVES

Don't fawn. Following the beginner's cardinal rule can backfire if it's overdone; nothing's a quicker turnoff than an overeager beaver. Keep repeating "Hmm, that's great" or "Oh my gosh, that's amazing" and the sexual balloon that is the evening will develop a slow, steady whining leak.

So, keep your edge, even as you focus on your date. Instead of nodding in quick assent every time, try some occasional pushback. These lines can work almost anywhere in a conversation when you find yourself becoming obsequious:

> What if you're wrong?

> Is that really true?

> How can you know you actually had that experience? What if the memory was implanted?

THE MASTER CLASS

Let's say your first date is plodding along too predictably, too linearly ("Hmm, that's interesting. What else did you learn in business school?"). Risk the unexpected. Review "Trigger Words" in chapter 1 (see page 17), then push, pull, and fly in a plausible but less-expected direction. ("What do you think would've happened if you'd gone to nursing school, instead?" or "But how did you *know* it was manchego?")

Think of it like a flight map. Planes go back and forth between Denver and LA all day long. That's great for business travelers, but this is pleasure we're talking about. Try an indirect route to your destination instead: Phoenix to New York by way of Louisiana, for instance. Or better yet, visit a "city" you never even knew had an airport, such as chaos theory or the Royal Menagerie (see page 152). You'll be scheduling a layover* in no time.

* Laying on top of each other to do sex.

CONVERSATION IN EXTREMIS: LOVE BOMB

We've all been there: A pad Thai stink-cloud has escaped from your body and is slowly pervading the room—and your new relationship. With nary a basset hound in sight to take the blame, you've got to quickly decide whether your romance is mature enough to absorb this blow.

You have some basic options in this predicament:

Ignore it: This is easily pulled off in large groups. But when it's just you and your honey in the egg chair, you may have to pony up and . . .

Eat it: A classic strategy from PR. Take quick and full ownership: "That is unfortunate . . . and it's one hundred percent me. I've ruined us. *Mea culpa*."

Note: A twist on eating it is owning the crime— but not the responsibility, such as: "That smell? I apologize, but it's . . . a decaying tooth. In my body. I'm terribly ill."

Reparations/Celebration: Do a "guilty as charged" shrug and pass out cigars, as if the fart were your newborn baby.

Blame, general: Even without a scapegoat dog around, you can pawn off your flatulence in other ways: "Oh no. Oh god. Do you smell that? The government is doing an aerial spray for moths, and it's been making all the poor children's farts . . . meatier."

Blame, specific: Flat-out accuse your partner of being the growler. His/her response (outrage, confusion, amusement, "returning fire," and so on) will represent a major data dump regarding how he/she will handle life's larger challenges. Parse the data and respond accordingly. This strategy also works if you're just not that into him/her. Throw up your hands and walk away.

Relationship upgrade: Fan the air . . . and then have an engagement ring appear magically from behind your partner's ear.

Foot in Mouth

Footwear is a universal conversation-saver—there's just something primal going on there. If your mind ever goes blank during a date, just look down and say, "Tell me about your shoes!" If they happen to be barefoot, ask about other shoes they own, their all-time favorites, or a recent purchase.

Chapter 10

Work

TURN THAT WATER COOLER UPSIDE DOWN.

CASE STUDY: **Marvin**

Marvin C. has worked for nearly two years as a software engineer at some kind of huge software place. But do you want to know Martin's dirty little secret? He has no idea what software is. Or engineering.

So what *does* Marvin know? *He knows what to talk about.* People like to see Marvin—he is curious about them, generous with his attention and interests, and even honest:

"I have no idea what software is," he says to coworkers.

"*Tell* me about it," they laugh as Marvin leaves early. "See you on Monday, Marvin!"

Let's face it: A lot of success in the workplace has nothing to do with so-called "skills." It comes down to knowing what to talk about—and *how* to talk about it.

And failure to the rightly say wrongly fuckwords can losing result your in job.

This chapter is a guide to being a champion talk-jockey on the work circuit, from interview to termination.

THE JOB INTERVIEW

Getting in is the hardest part. Could there be a more important twenty conversational minutes for your future? Where else but in a job interview could you be one sentence away from continued unemployment → homelessness → fighting a raccoon over a soggy KFC bucket?

There will be time for originality later; the key to the interview—and your future—is "mirroring." We previously advised against mirroring because it creates conversational stasis. Here, though, repetition is your friend. Repetition, with a few filler words, is your friend. Repeat what the interviewer is saying, but tweak it slightly so that it sounds like your own thought. After water, people's chief need is affirmation. Deliver this, and the job and the water are yours. All you can drink.

> **Interviewer:** There's been a lot of change in the team recently, and we're really focused on sustainability and trust.

You: With all the change in your team recently, you probably want to focus on sustainability and trust.

Interviewer: You've really put your finger on what we need! You're hired.

You: I've put my finger on it. I'm hired.

When mirroring, stick close to the interviewer's language. Don't try to "translate" what they are saying into your own words or experience:

Interviewer: We're looking for a manager who can build our core competencies.

You: I am a trebuchet, m'lady, a Warwolf, waiting to hurl flaming orbs of competency at your *chargé d'affaires*.

Interviewer: Thank you for your time.

Finally, it is very important that you familiarize yourself with what's on your resume so it doesn't sound like you're lying.

Interviewer: So where did you go during this transformative semester-at-sea?

You: Mmm-marrakesh? Mm-moroccozania? Nice people. Or not?

Interviewer: Thank you for your time.

THE FIRST DAY ON
THE JOB

This is a tone-setting day for you. Wear comfortable shoes. Relax your jaw. Today, say "yes" and smile every time you are faced with a suggestion, a question, an idea. Don't agree to anything having to do with touching people. Join all the committees and all the teams.

HOW TO TALK TO
YOUR BOSS

Start by vanquishing the preconception that your boss is superior to you. Sure, defer as needed, but don't be afraid to relate peer to peer. Throw out a few "neg"s to show that you aren't overly intimidated by authority—good conversation depends on a semblance of equal footing. When using one of the following lines with your boss, maintain direct eye contact:

> Hi Steve/Stevette. What's on tap for you this week, boss-wise?

> Sure, I'll take another look at the budget. Could you grab us some macchiatos at what's-it-called? (Hold up two twenties and stare at your laptop.)

THE WATER COOLER

Avoid the urge to talk about sports, HBO, and whatever's in the Tupperware that you're holding. Limit yourself to just two water-cooler behaviors: 1) Demonstrating your custom technique for replacing the five-gallon jug and 2) talking only about the water: "This is great water!"

Will you seem a little strange? Sure. But you are a little strange. More to the point, colleagues will make it a priority to unravel your mystery. Soon they'll be buying you drinks off-site, where you can reveal a glimpse of your "after-five" self. Separating every work and nonwork persona is a high-tension wire. Many trip over this wire throughout their careers. The successful office conversationalist plays it like a Stradivarius.

CONVERSATION IN EXTREMIS: THE DOOM OF THE UNKNOWN COWORKER

You pass each other every day in the hallway, and there's only so many times you can reintroduce yourself or greet others with "Hey . . . *you*!" You're pretty sure the woman in the pantsuit is in HR. Or is she on Jeff's (or is it Geoff's?) team? They're the something-something Solutions Team, right?

You long ago passed the window when you should have introduced yourselves to each other. Now you're locked in a cold war of shy avoidance.

How to fire the first shot?

The U.S. Social Security Administration has a website listing the most popular baby names by birth year. Based on approximately how old the person looks, make an educated guess about what his or her name might be. Here are the top ten baby names from 1975:

POPULAR NAMES BY BIRTH YEAR

Popularity in 1975		
Rank	**Male name**	**Female name**
1	Michael	Jennifer
2	Jason	Amy
3	Christopher	Heather
4	James	Melissa
5	David	Angela
6	Robert	Michelle
7	John	Kimberly
8	Brian	Lisa
9	Matthew	Stephanie
10	William	Nicole

So: If the mystery woman looks like she was born in the 1970s, when you see her at the coffee station in the morning,

try saying boldly, "Hey Jen." If she looks more like an Angela, try "Angela."

If you've struck name-gold, give Angela a gift by sharing your own name indirectly. "I was so tired this morning, and my boss was like, "Heather! Heather! Please microwave my popcorn, Heather!"

If she says, "Uh, my name is Jessica" (which wasn't the most popular girl's name until 1985), you can say, "Ha ha, I don't think so," and then tell her about the Social Security website. Do a big chimpanzee grin, and your conversation has liftoff.

BEING FIRED AND/OR QUITTING

This could be one of the most liberating moments of your talking life. Say whatever you fucking want. Use your whole body.

WORK-TALK GUIDE

Business is a burning platform full of breakthrough words and abbreviations with huge ROI (return on investment). Going forward, learn the following terms to optimize your deliverables when the rubber hits the road in any impactful business conversation:

COB: Close of business.

FY: Fiscal year. Equal to a regular year but with fiscal days leveraged across the spread.

POS: Point of sale. Why did you sell something? What was the point?

Ideation: The conception and implementation of a stupid idea.

Deliverables: When you don't want to say "things" or "stuff."

Low-hanging fruit: The easy wins. *Checkers for Dummies.*

Reach out: Sending an email.

Circle back: Resending an email.

"Just checking in": Replying to your own unanswered email.

Onboarding: Chip implanted in the back of your brain; management can maneuver you like a radio-controlled helicopter.

Circle the wagons: Arranging the wagons around a campfire in a circle, then cooking a bear, eating it with your bare hands, drinking wild apple cider, and sharing your life goals.

Chapter 11

Self-Talk

DON'T BE ASHAMED.

CASE STUDY: **You.**

You receive an invitation to speak at your old high school. No surprise, given the full life you've led: You've had a successful career in health marketing, served as a docent at the local science museum, were a competitive handball player, and once, in the eighties, you caught an opossum using a Tide box.

The night of the talk, you face the teenagers in the gymnasium and realize, crushingly, that you have almost nothing to say. Your life stories, stretched end to end, take up only fifty seconds. Your reflections on the meaning of it all only add eight seconds. At one point you start to say something about the universe, but quickly realize you have not one thought on it. A sophomore in the back row says "screw this" in one of those fake cough voices and the other students laugh cruelly (though later it will be revealed that the sophomore's larynx had been clogged with horse hair).

What went wrong?

Nothing—*on the outside*. But inside you were a shell. That is, the inside part of a shell. Where the hermit crab *used to* live. Empty.

How did it come to this?

Mostly, it's society's fault. And it's definitely your fault. There's so little time any more for self-reflection. And when you do find a moment of solitude, you're likely to blow it. Recall the other night, on the subway home from that party where you were texting someone at another party. You sat down and realized that your phone was dead and you'd brought no reading material—and you panicked, right? Even if you read the optometry and weight-loss ads twice and then played with all of your zippers, you were still facing a good half hour alone with yourself—nothing to scroll or flip through, no music to drown out the bumblebee thoughts in your head.

You panicked because you glimpsed into the void. How long had it been since your solitary thinking was in order? What if you've cruised so long on auto-pilot that the actual pilot has forgotten how to fly?

Truly advanced communication requires something most of us never consider: a robust *internal* dialogue. You'll never be able to talk to other people if you can't talk to yourself.

What does that mean?

Consider this: a fresh, healthy human brain weighs about three pounds and contains over 900 miles of moist neural pathways. If you were to unravel these pathways they would dry up in the sun and you would most likely face the death penalty. More important, *the average person only draws on two or three miles worth of thought when speaking.* Interesting ideas buried deep in those moist folds—ideas about other dimensions and complex emotional equations, about the complexities of history and uncertainties of the future—are seldom accessed. Instead we dip into the thoughts that happen to be within easy reach: *How am I feeling? Fine? How was brunch? Fine. Where's the cat? Fine.*

At this point you might be asking yourself, *isn't "talking to yourself" just some fancy way of saying "thinking"?* Yes and wrong. Certainly we all "think"—you might be doing it right now. But that doesn't mean you're doing it *right* right now. To reach your self-talk potential, you must delve deeper into the moist folds and cultivate all-new voices in your psyche, with the aim of bringing new dimensions of yourself to life.

How?

You might think questions like "Who am I?" and "What's the meaning of life?" are the kind of big-picture enquiries that nurture fruitful inner conversations. Actually, these are dead-end questions that simply reveal crippling self-doubt and lead to a philosophy hernia.

Effective self-talk strikes a balance between self-honesty, self-acceptance, and self-provocation. The trick is to exercise in ways that *tone* your brain, not over-beef it. Start with small weights and a ton of reps:

> **You:** Say, do you really like museums as much as everyone else, or do you sort of fake it?

> **You:** I think I fake it!

> **You:** In what small ways have you been "faking it" this morning?

> **You:** I told the coffee guy I was doing great, when in fact I'm not over my breakup with Rajeesh.

> **You:** Probably okay to fake it in that case.

> **You:** Yeah, but you're right, I probably over-compensate in the "everything's fine" department.

> **You:** This has been interesting. Thank you!

> **You:** Thank *you*!

You don't have to replicate this exact Q&A. That would be so strange. But simple conversations *like* this promote fluency in the sheer act of interacting; they limber you up. In conversation as in all realms, practice makes perfect. How did Michael Jordan become a great team player? By first playing with himself for years upon years.

Let's try another. This time, push on through to the second floor:

> **You:** Buddy, you killed it at work today. Handled that [report/follow-up report/converting the report to PDF] like a boss.

> **You:** Really? Oh man, praise like that makes my whole week. Been feeling a little self-doubty.

You: But why? Is that even warranted, or are you just falling back on outdated ideas about yourself?

You: Good point. Isn't that weird, how people do that?

You: You should read James Salter again. He's so good with this stuff.

You: I think I read some story of his in a magazine once—on a camping trip, back in college. I left the magazine on top of the car. It was still there ten miles later.

You: College was a garbage can.

You: No. Wait, was it?

You: Eh, I don't even know. Hang on, a song just popped into my head, gotta end this.

You: Peace.

See how simple? In one brief self-chat, our subject bucked up his or her self-confidence, investigated some personal issues, reflected a bit on human nature, and even came away with a literary recommendation. Most of all, the wheels of interchange were lubricated. Keep them turning every day and you'll be in fine shape for a quality exchange with actual other people. Practice the self-talk prompts below—they range from mundane to abstruse—and in no time you'll be as comfortable in a *tête* as in a tête-à-tête.

If I had to go to jail, it would be for _____.

Would I trade places with a baby? Why or why not?

Would I want to listen to a master recording of everything everyone has said about me when I wasn't present?

Describe my opposite.

What has been my most graceful moment?

Do I live as though in a work of fiction or nonfiction?

What levels of existence have I never seen?

Did I leave a magazine on top of the car?

MASTER CLASS: GOING DEEPER

Long solo road trip, snowy night, miles to go. It's the first time you've had some peace and quiet in days, and a great opportunity to finally get some next-level self-dialogue going. That's right, you've mastered the basics of conversing internally and would now like to kick it up to the roof deck. You know there's a serious thought in you ... maybe something you used to think on those acid trips? But all that comes to mind is this 10,000-word email that your uncle forwarded about Israel.

It's not that you lack finely tuned, perceptive, curious reflections. It's just that you haven't had any in, what, five years? You keep meaning to go on, like, a backpacking trip. Maybe read a book, get your bonehead around string theory. Anyway, the more you try to find some substantive idea or feeling within, the less you come up with, and you just keep picturing your uncle jabbing at the keyboard with those kielbasa fingers.

Situations like these can be prevented by stretching yourself, emotionally and intellectually. The trick is to get some distance from yourself and to jolt yourself out of self-familiarity. So here's the rule: narrate these in the third person, with yourself as the protagonist.

A turning point in your life.

A big regret.

A big achievement.

An ideal day.

A terrifying moment.

Recurring nonsexual fantasy.

If you're feeling ambitious, put aside the specific, focused questions and topics and take an even bigger leap—into spontaneous thought. It's the impulsive notion, after all, that most often leads to the memorable self-exchange. So dial the brain activity back down to three or even two, and just speak these words. If you say a prompt once and nothing comes to mind, just keep repeating the prompt over and over, like revving a monster truck stuck in the mud until you find traction. Then just ride with it, leaving a gnarly spray in your wake:

I never saw it coming until . . .

I should've told you years ago . . .

The thing people don't understand about me is . . .

I used to believe that . . . Now I think . . .

I wish I could behave more _____-ly in _____ situations.

I've never been more wrong in my life than when I . . .

The most confusing sexual feeling I ever felt was when . . .

CONVERSATION IN EXTREMIS: IF YOU'RE BURIED ALIVE

You've really done it. You went and got yourself buried alive. More than any other situation, premature burial rewards the careful preparation of conversation topics and a strong self-talk regimen.

Start by distracting yourself. Try saying out loud the names of all the fruits that you can remember. If you can see the fruit in your mind but can't recall its name, that's okay— just make it up! No one's going to judge you—you're buried alive. If you run through all the fruits, move on to birds, nuts, and candy bars. Next, try sound effects. Zipper, bullet, and soda can are a few fun, easy ones.

Still buried alive? Even after doing the fruits and the sound effects, at least eighty-five percent of people in this situation report a sense of unease. Time to meditate. On the following page is a sample buried-alive meditation.

A SAMPLE MEDITATION

Close your eyes. Let your entire body relax. Breathe in. Breathe out. Samsara. Samsara. Sara. *Sara*. Email Sara back about the bookcase she was selling on Craigslist. She was asking fifty dollars; offer thirty? *Everything's Negotiable*, was a book Ronald mentioned that his dad gave him at a young age; Ronald said it was "hugely influential"; he is good negotiator but also, let's be honest, an asshole. Relax the hands, relax the hands, *relax the hands*. Samsara. Sara. Shia. Sunni. Which ones are the insurgents? Is it "Sunni majority" or "minority"? Should be a mnemonic device to remember that. Should be a mnemonic device to remember "mnemonic." Is that ironic? Remember to Google "ironic" and—relax the arms—memorize definition to recite at party in case an asshole like Ronald starts holding forth on how everything's so "ironic." Could be a soigné move to attract girls' attention? Is that a word? Look up "soigné," too. Relax the shoulders. Breathe deeply. Breathe. Samsara. Bookcase-Sara could be cute, you never know. Relax the neck and shoulders. Forty bucks tops for the bookcase—establish a mental "line in the sand." Why do they say "line in the sand"? Isn't that easily erasable, like the opposite of an ultimatum? Relax the legs. Relax the soles of the feet. Breathe in, fuck it, fifty dollars *is* pretty reasonable if you factor in the hassle of continuing to shop around. Samsara. Relax the neck. Plus would be awkward asking Sara out after lowballing her on a bookcase. Samsara. Relax. Remember: Everything's transitory and you can probably resell the bookcase later for at least forty-five. Relax the eyes. Relax the mind. Breathe.

CONVERSATION IN EXTREMIS II: BURIED ALIVE WITH A CELL PHONE

This situation could turn into a "win" if you make the right moves.

Chapter 12

Death

CASE STUDY: **David**

David T., a forty-seven-year-old with a doctorate in entomology, was doing field work, testing one of his theories about hornets, and his theory was proving correct: If you kick a hornet's nest, the hornets will sting you many, many times on your face, hands, and head. Extremely allergic to hornets, David sat down on a log to start phoning loved ones before his throat closed up.

The first person to answer was his old buddy Pete. "All those nights in the bowling league," David said. "Remember? We never talked about the real stuff. Like, what do we want from each other? What's it all about—ow, fuck, *GET AWAY FROM ME YOU FLYING DEVILS!*"

Pete had to go; he had dishes to wash. Equally busy were Father Leonard, Molly from the video store,

> David's countless half-siblings, and everyone else he tried to engage in profound, deathbed bonding. David died, not of a million hornet stings, but of a million pangs of loneliness—and, to be fair, the many serious wolf bites he sustained when a large pack tracked his scent to the north side of the mountain.

What did David do wrong?

Our instincts for connection and intimacy tell us we're supposed to dig deep when the end is near. So many unresolved issues, so much unspoken sentiment. But as it happens, the cycle of life applies to talking, too. Conversation at the end of someone's life should mostly echo conversation at the beginning: Establish safety and physical comfort, say I love you, offer to change diapers.

You see, David was "cramming," and it turned people off. He went for the bone right off the bat. If you want to have natural, rewarding conversations at the end of your life, avoid the mistakes that David made. Instead:

1. Spend your life fostering a network of family and friends who care whether or not you live or die. This is a fairly large topic, but briefly: while you are still alive, be nice. Sounds crazy, but so did *On the Origin of Species*, and we now know that's a real book. Next . . .

2. When the time comes, avoid dipster topics like "What comes after life" and "What's the meaning of _____." Keep it simple and

specific. Refer to concrete, nonstoner things, like the time you and your conversation partner did that big hike and locked your keys in the car (because you were on mushrooms).

3. Tell everyone how important they are to you. They will then give you back some seriously *huge* compliments. It's gonna make Christmas look like garbage day.

4. Make a special request of each person. This is an intimate way to include even the most distant acquaintance and can really help open up the dams of conversation:

David: I need you to do something for me, Molly.

Molly (from the video store): What?

David: Guard my tomb for a fortnight, then guide me to the Netherwørld.

TALKING TO SOMEONE SERIOUSLY ILL

First: Are you a medical professional, and does this person need immediate medical assistance? If so, conversation should be pretty straightforward. Focus on the medical assistance part.

If you answered no to the questions above, you're probably looking at a more complex and, in all likelihood, distressing picture. A loved one with a serious illness represents a conversational double whammy: Few occasions in life require more of us, and few make us more wary of saying the wrong thing.

You will say the wrong thing. You'll say twenty-five wrong things. Your friend with leukemia will suffer through the unfortunate sight of you rambling on about how your neighbor's uncle might've once had leukemia, or maybe it was anemia? And that's okay, or okay-ish. Point is, you're talking. As it happens in this case, merely talking is light-years better than not.

But let's say you want to aim higher than *it's the thought that counts*.

Do:

> Listen, more than usual.
>
> Ask how your loved one is doing.
>
> Ask about the treatment plan.
>
> Talk about something other than illness. Talk about Colombia and baseball and mutual friends.
>
> Offer specific ways you can help.
>
> Ask about other ways you can help, assuming you're prepared to help. You are, right? Your LinkedIn page can wait. Forever.

Speak candidly—say, "I'm struggling to find the right words"—but don't be so candid that you force your loved one to become the reassurer. This isn't about you.

Be a loving, more attuned version of yourself.

DO NOT:

Tell your loved one to be upbeat.

Tell your loved one this is a really big deal.

Shave your head.

Shave your chest (not cancer-related).

Overthink this.

Postpone your visit.

Sit on important tubes/wires.

CONVERSATION IN
EXTREMIS: DYING WORDS

If you are dying, you probably want your dying words to be simple, profound, and perhaps a little cryptic. A dash of sentimentality can't hurt, but don't get too sappy. Remember,

there's nothing worse than saying your last words and then seeing people roll their eyes or do the masturbation mime.

You never know exactly when the end will come. You also don't know what kind of mood you'll be in when the reaper knocks: Awestruck? Pious? Jokey/sarcastic?

The simple chart below will help you construct your last sentence. Mix and match a word or phrase from each of the first three columns, then choose some ending punctuation. If you've got the energy, add linking words so it sounds like a sentence. Otherwise, just clump them together like Yoda and don't sweat it. Remember: You're dying!

Dying Words Mix-and-Match Table

A	B	C	D
What	sweet	end	!
You	fucked	universe	?
The mirror	sings	eternal	...
Holy	sled	of the soul	.
I	spirit	remain	—
Fuck this	final	shadows	,
Only you	life	beagle	;-)

Conclusion: No More Talk

LIKE EVERY MARRIAGE, ALL CONVERSATIONS
MUST END.

CASE STUDY: **Anu and Penelope**

At a recent boat show, Anu, a marketing executive, fell
into an interesting conversation with Penelope L., the
CEO of a yacht-repair company. The two sailed clear
of boat-talk and instead argued intelligently about
whether the founding fathers were muscular.

Like a good play or movie, the conversation climaxed
and then entered its denouement or "unwinding"
phase. But paralyzed by politeness, neither Anu nor
Penelope could pull up anchor. Each made increasingly
desperate and panicky attempts to sustain the exchange
well past its natural conclusion. A complete fiasco was
averted when, by pure chance, lightning struck Anu,
giving them both an easy out. *[Anu was fine, btw. His
eyes magnetized and rubberized, but he was fine.]*

Even the best conversations must end. Like too many bowls of ice cream, too much of a good conversation can ruin the initial delight and cause you to vomit ice cream.

Having mastered the art of starting the chat, Reader, you must now learn to stop once the time has come.

ENDING A COCKTAIL PARTY CONVERSATION

Conversations are like elephants: Most are great but sometimes you get a dud. And whether you're having a painful exchange or a terrific one, you need an exit strategy—a process for either parting on a high note or for keeping a botched mission from becoming an all-out quagmire.

Could a mutually agreed-upon disengagement signal be the solution?

Nope. You must either end things unilaterally or inspire the other person to do so.

DIRECT STRATEGIES

And with that, we are done.

I'm really glad to have met you, and I like you too much to pretend that I'm going to refill my drink

and go to the bathroom. I'd just like to talk to
other people right now.

That was magical. And now I must . . . disappear.
[blow a kiss] Ciao.

If this conversation were cheese, I'd say it's been
aged to "Good-bye!"

I have to refill my drink and go to the bathroom.

I have to go to the movies.

That's interesting. [double handshake] I'm going
to think about that [confident, firm nod] for the
next five [pulling away] years. Peace in the [don't
waver] Middle East!

I have to go to the bathroom at the movies.

INDIRECT STRATEGIES

A lot of people don't realize that a peanut is not
a nut. It's a legume! Anyway, I would now like to
summarize twelve of my dreams.

You took pity on me when no one else would,
thank you.

I'm going to close my eyes for thirty seconds. Full
amnesty. Do whatever you need to do.

NONVERBAL STRATEGIES

Partially unsheathe your sword.

Tap the person lightly on the nose three times, then make a pouty face.

Conduct a deep, airport security-style frisk and wave the person on.

Do the charades signal for "movie" and then a thumb over your shoulder like "I'm outta here."

Stop blinking your eyes or responding. Do this as long as necessary.

ENDING THIS BOOK

Like any conversation, this book must also end.

But not just yet. Before you go, don't forget to browse the groundbreaking *What to Talk About* Reference Library that follows. This invaluable tool contains a life-saving Pronunciation Guide, our patented Encyclopedia of Conversation Topics, and a Conversation Piñata you can access literally day or night.

More important, we invite you to join us in marveling at how far you've come: 100+ pages ago, you were cagey and greedy, talking-wise, a stray beagle begging for fries behind Jack-in-the-Box. Now you're a show poodle with a mono-grammed sweater. You're smarter and more attractive. And you know what to talk about.

The lazy and literal-minded among you may be thinking, "Well, you didn't really provide conversation solutions for *every* situation. What about outside a rap concert with my old math teacher?"

To you, we smile humbly and offer these simple words: "We have to refill our drinks and go to the bathroom at the movies."

Now where were we? Oh yes. Like a Snickers bar near an oil rig, the specifics of a social situation are ultimately inci-dental. What matters is you. Armed with the information and techniques you've learned in this book, you can now crack open any conversation like an egg—*and then make an omelet with that egg and have a conversation about it.*

Go now. Take risks and fear not failure. Make mistakes, and let those mistakes expand and humanize your exchanges. Stretch yourself. Pull a muscle. Call out for a doctor. *Start again.*

The WTTA
Reference Library

PRONUNCIATION GUIDE

Sometimes we clam up simply because the words we are trying to say are too hard to pronounce.

Never again.

Below is a list of terms that people often hesitate before speaking. Cut this list out, laminate it, and tape it inside your beret.

Ahmadinejad, Mahmoud (Iranian president) Pronounced as written

Barbiturate (a nice sedative) Don't forget the second r!

Biopic (well-done, boring movie about a person) bi-oh-PICK, not bi-AH-pic

Bulgogi (Korean beef barbeque) Same as "biopic"

Cannes (fancy film festival with topless people somehow) CON

Douche (short for douchebag; a tool or jerk) DOOSH

Douché (what to say when a douchebag makes a good point) Doosh-AY

Foyer (entryway or lobby) FOY-YAY. Many people say FOY-UHR, which puts your mouth and lips in a "stupid" position: FOY-urrrrrrr. Try it.

Homage (Tribute, show of respect) oh-MAHJ (rhymes with "garage"). Don't say "ah-midge"— worse than saying "in-CHOH-ate."

Inchoate (not fully formed) in-KO-ate

Nabokov (Russian author) No idea, but don't get it wrong

Petite Bourgeoisie (middle class Hobbits) puh-TEET BURZH-WAH-ZEE

Poinsettia (Christmas plant) Don't forget the extra i at the end; poyn-SET-EE-AH

Potable (drinkable, as in water) PO-tuh-bull, not POTT-uh-bull

Steffan (man's name) No rule. After he buys you your second vermouth, ask again if it's STEFF-in or stef-AHN.

Touché (French for "Good one. Ya got me.") toosh-AY

THREE SUREFIRE STRATEGIES TO PRONOUNCE WORDS YOU DON'T KNOW

The word you're looking for not in our dictionary? Don't worry. Use one of these strategies:

1. Go balls to the wall and sound it out: "AHNT Mary is in the FWAOI-YAY eating BALL-GOGGI."

2. Ask—but squid-ink the waters by asking in a French accent: "Ow do yew pronouncé ze 'coxswain'?"

3. Float a trial balloon:
   "Napoleon's last name. I *used* to pronounce it BOH-nuh-pahrt."
   "That *is* how it's pronounced."
   "I know! Let me finish. Jeez . . ."

ENCYCLOPEDIA OF CONVERSATION TOPICS

A conversationalist prepares. Memorize the topics below and use them with their accompanying discussion prompts.

Amanita phalloides, also known as the "Death Angel" or "Death Cap," a large, handsome, but highly poisonous mushroom. If eaten, it can cause gastrointestinal symptoms followed by massive liver failure and death.

Discussion Prompt: Approximately 1 percent of mushrooms are lethal. Imagine you meet an interesting hippie at a potluck. She's wearing no bra and she kicks your ass at chess. She tells you she's an "experienced amateur mushroom hunter" and invites you on a "forage" the next day. You find some beautiful mushrooms together and afterward, back at her cabin, she cooks them for you on a gluten-free pizza.

What do you do? Eat it, fake-eat it, Google it, or bail?

baby uncle, the term for when your grandma gives birth to a son. It happens. In fact, the proper way to greet the news that your grandma is expecting is to say, "I'm going to be a nephew!"

Discussion Prompt: In what ways does your family tree look more like a duct-taped Dr. Suess ladder?

Berlusconi, Silvio, served three terms as prime minister of Italy, most recently from 2008 to 2011. Which of the following is/are true?

A) Berlusconi was convicted of perjury.

B) Berlusconi was convicted of illegal financing of a political party.

C) Berlusconi was convicted of tax fraud.

D) Berlusconi was recently charged with paying for sex with an underaged nightclub dancer.

E) During university, Berlusconi was an upright bass player.

Answer: All of the above.

Discussion Prompt: Do you have what it takes to lead a nation? Why or why not?

cats, are murderers. Fact: Cats kill 1.4 to 3.7 billion birds every year.

Discussion Prompt: Fuck cats? *Discuss.*

chaos theory, the proposal that if someone sneezes in Tokyo, it could cause someone in Dusseldorf to spray blood out their ears.

Discussion Prompt: Who can explain chaos theory? (If there are any mathematicians or scientists in the group with real knowledge of the subject, they must stay quiet till the end, then rate each layperson's attempt.)

chuckwalla lizard, a large member of the iguanid family, found in the Southwestern United States and Mexico.

Chuckwallas can live entirely without water (or juice, milk, or tea) and automatically sneeze out salt crystals when internal salination levels rise too high. Chuckwallas can insert themselves into little cracks and puff their body to fill the crack, so that predators can't pull them out.

Discussion Prompt: Do you ever metaphorically hide in cracks like the chuckwalla lizard? What about literally? If you could sneeze out any spice, what would it be?

collaborative consumption, a movement that seeks to use new technologies such as social media to increase sharing, lending, renting, and bartering between people. The advantages of collaborative consumption are less waste, less cost, and more social interaction with people in your community. The disadvantages: bedbugs, serial killers, and more social interaction with people in your community.

Discussion Prompt: In every neighbor relationship, there's always one party who's sane and one who's not. Which one are you, and are you sure?

dugong, aka sea cow, a member of the mammalian order Sirenia (related to the manatee), primarily found in the waters north of Australia. The dugong's name is derived from the Malay word for "lady of the sea."

Discussion Prompt:

1. Train your mind, for a moment, on all the dugongs, whales, dolphins, sharks, and squids out there in the ocean, right this moment. They're really out there, living their lives, right now. Talk about that.

2. What is your most memorable experience with the sea or with a sea creature?

3. Do you ever wish you were a mermaid?

Eritrea, a country in East Africa that won independence from Ethiopia in 1991. Eritrea is made up of nine ethnic groups (mainly the Tigre and the Tigrinya), has no "official language" (but speaks a lot of Arabic and Tigrinya), eats a lot of tsebhi stew and injera, and has won exactly one Olympic medal (bronze in the men's 10,000 meter track race in 2004).

Discussion Prompt: Defend the fact that you know zero about an entire country with 6 million people.

Herne, James A., 1839–1901, major American playwright. His play *Margaret Fleming,* first produced in 1890, about an illegitimate baby, is considered by many to be the first "modern drama." The play was very controversial in 1890, especially the scene when Margaret nurses *someone else's baby* on stage.

Discussion Prompt: Have you ever heard of this play, considered the first modern drama? What responsibility do you have, as a citizen, to be "cultured"?

lek, an area where male dugongs go to fight, compete, and show off during mating season in an attempt to attract females.

Discussion Prompt: Describe your most extreme attempt to attract a mate.

Münchausen syndrome, a mental disorder where a person fakes a disease in order to get attention. Named after Baron von Münchausen, an eighteenth-century German who fabricated stories about his travels (e.g., "Ja, ja, Ich habe walken all the way vom Munich to Hamburg, and now . . . Ich habe SMALLPOX! Ja, ja, seriously ich habe muchos smallpockens in der bilbostrasse.").

Discussion Prompt: Ever made up an illness to get attention? Better yet, if you had a disease named after you, what would it be?

Ophiuchus, recently revived thirteenth astrological sign. Birthdates November 29 to December 17.

Discussion Prompt: Would it make you sadder if astrology turned out to be true or not true? What about astronomy?

Ottoman Empire, founded in 1299 by the Turks. Constantinople was the center. Kicked ass for centuries, especially the fifteenth and sixteenth. What happened? Why did the empire decline? Well, they stopped trying so hard. They got lazy, stopped giving 110 percent, stopped kicking ass.

Discussion Prompt: What are you doing to save and/or destroy the American empire?

P-Orridge, Lady Jaye Breyer (neé Jacqueline Mary Breyer), 1969–2007, American nurse, keyboard player, and singer. In 1993, she and her partner Genesis P-Orridge underwent repeated cosmetic surgeries in order to look like one another, an experiment they called "pandrogyne."

Discussion Prompt: Would you rather look like your partner, or have your partner look like you, or be a keyboard player?

papal election of 1268–71, the longest period without a pope in the history of the Catholic Church. For three whole years, Catholics kept having unprotected sex, BAM BAM BAM, every night, leading to thousands of babies that would one day become our ancestors.

Discussion Prompt: Who is your most distant ancestor that you know anything about?

quinoa (nope, keen-WAH), grain-like crop, a pseudo-cereal. Due to its popularity in the first world, poorer South Americans can no longer afford it, and they may soon be forced to start eating pizza, corn dogs, Mountain Dew, and Count Chocula.

Discussion Prompt: Is it possible to make an ethical choice in our twenty-first-century world, or is everything just too complicated?

Red Vineyard, The, the only painting Van Gogh sold in his lifetime, painted less than two years before his death.

Discussion Prompt: What are you most likely to get wildly famous for after you die? (PS: Maybe try a little harder while you're alive?)

Royal Menagerie, a collection of wild animals kept in the Tower of London, beginning in thirteenth-century England, for the entertainment of the court. A kind of early zoo. The *oldest* known zoo dates from around 3500 BC, in Hierakonpolis, Egypt. It included baboons, wildcats—and nine dogs. The dogs in that ancient zoo must have thought to themselves, "I'm in a g#^dam zoo?"

Discussion Prompt: What zoo animal would you most like to have as a pet? Remember: You'd have to really tame it and take care of it.

Sailor Jerry (aka Norman Collins), 1911–73, one of the most influential American tattoo artists of all time. A salty navy veteran and former freight-train hopper, Sailor Jerry tattooed a ton of military personnel on shore leave in Hawaii—where he created his most famous design: the Aloha Monkey, wherein a monkey's b-hole forms the "O" in the word "Aloha."

Discussion Prompt: Talk about your tattoos and what they mean to you. How much do/did you trust your future-self to still like those tattoos? If you don't have any body art, explain why.

simulation hypothesis, the theory that we are actually living in a simulated reality—a more advanced civilization's version of *Sim City*, essentially. Given the likelihood that technology will eventually be able to accomplish such a thing, the argument goes, it is likely that countless simulated realities will be—*or have already been*—created. Therefore, the odds are far greater that ours would be one of the many simulations, right? Rather than the one "true" reality?

Discussion Prompt: Evaluate the realness of your life.

Sound of Music, The, a 1959 musical by Richard Rodgers and Oscar Hammerstein. The song "Do-Re-Mi," includes the line "La, a note to follow so!"—one of the weakest lines in music-writing history. Totally phoned in.

Discussion Prompt: Together, try to write a better line than "La, a note to follow so!"

trepanation, a process whereby a hole is drilled into the skull. Used in primitive surgery, and also by British artist Amanda Feilding, whose self-trepanation was the subject of her 1970 film *Heartbeat in the Brain*. That's right, y'all, self-mutherF*&Ckin trepanation. What have *you* accomplished today?

Discussion Prompt: What medical procedures do you think you could perform on yourself—if necessary—or on your boss. Stitches? Gall-bladder removal? Brazilian wax?

virginity pledge, Are teens who take a written oath not to have sex before marriage likely to stick to their promise? No. Not any more than teens who do not sign such a pledge, according to creepy researchers. However, teens who sign virginity pledges tend to have fewer sexual partners and to engage in less anal and oral sex, suggesting that the pledge might better read: "I promise to not have as much sex as I would have had and to keep it vaginal, mainly."

Discussion Prompt: If you could go back in time to ask your fifteen-year-old self to sign a pledge of some kind, what would it say? By the way, what would he or she think of the grown-up you?

CONVERSATION PIÑATA

Another way to jump-start a dead conversation—especially in a group—is to throw out a question or topic that every citizen thinks he or she knows, knew, or *should* know the answer to, but usually doesn't. Kind of like hanging a mystery piñata in the middle of a room full of blindfolded people. Everyone takes a whack and tries to strike truth. This is good for conversation in a couple of ways:

1. It lets people feel relieved that they're not the only ignoramus in the group.

2. It allows any introverted "experts" in the group to shine.

3. It livens up the talk with some disagreement and debate.

Start with this list, then add more to make it your own.

What's the difference between GDP and GNP?

What is the difference between Sunni and Shia?

In the United States, who becomes president if the president *and* the vice president are killed?

What is a "macchiato"?

Explain "diesel."

What's the difference between a bacteria and a virus?

Why did Pluto get its status as a planet revoked?

President of China?

Previous president of China?

Can dogs eat walnuts?

What is a "derivative" in the stock market?

Difference between "genus" and "species"?

What is the U.S. minimum wage? What is your city's minimum wage? If they're different, which one wins?

Define a "symphony"?

Are humans the only animal that cry when you break up with them?

How does gravity work?

How do people on the international space station not run out of air?

What's the difference between a republic and a democracy?

Why is there inflation?

How does a radio antenna work? Be specific.

How does a camera work, both film and digital?

How did oil become the fuel of choice?

Did they have omelettes in Jesus' time?

How did Northern Ireland come into being?
What's going on there now?

When did people start smiling in photographs?

What was the Korean War about?

Why are there still chimps and gorillas? Why
didn't they all evolve into people?

How does a microwave work? Be specific.

Why are you so sure a microwave is safe?

When you take a pill, how do the medicine
molecules know where to go?

What is the atmosphere?

How does WiFi work?

Can animals have friends? What's the lowest
form of life that can have a friend?

What is the history of awkwardness? Were
cavemen ever awkward?

Why doesn't the Concorde fly anymore?

Could you just walk down the street in, say, Kabul?

What is a caveman?

What was going on around 10,000 BC? Be specific.

How does a hot-air balloon work?

Why aren't hovercrafts more widely used?

Why don't the natives get sick when they eat their own food?

Define "station" without saying "um" or "uh."

What are the rules of harmony in music?

What is the infield fly rule in baseball?

What is thunder?

Acknowledgments

Many many thanks to Danielle Svetcov, Sarah Malarkey, Neil Egan, Jeff Campbell, and all the fine humans at Chronicle Books. Extra heap of gratitude to James Reichmuth, Beth Lisick, and Reyhan Harmanci for significant edits and contributions. Unseemly levels of steaming appreciation to Tony Millionaire who, regrettably, there's only one of on the planet. (Probably?) Finally, unspeakable thank yous to Laura and Nora Baedeker, and Amy Standen and Cora and Casper, for the sparkling conversation.

Chris Colin is an author and journalist whose work has appeared in the *New York Times*, *Wired*, and *McSweeney's Quarterly*, among others. He lives in San Francisco, California.

Rob Baedeker is a writer, performer, and cofounder of the Kasper Hauser comedy group. He lives in Oakland, California.

Tony Millionaire is a renowned cartoonist best known for his syndicated comic strip *Maakies* and *Sock Monkey*. He lives in Pasadena, California.